BRIDGES

A LIFE BUILDING & CROSSING THEM

DR. IRENE TROWELL-HARRIS,

MAJOR GENERAL, USAF (RETIRED)

PUBLISHED BY

FORTIS

A NONFICTION IMPRINT FROM ADDUCENT
Adducent, Inc.
www.Adducent.co

TITLES DISTRIBUTED IN
North America
United Kingdom
Western Europe
South America
Australia

BRIDGES

A Life Building & Crossing Them

Dr. Irene Trowell-Harris

BRIDGES

A Life Building & Crossing Them
Dr. Irene Trowell-Harris

ISBN: 9781937592509 (hardback)

Published by Adducent, Inc. under its Fortis nonfiction imprint
Jacksonville, Florida
www.Adducent.Co

Published in the United States of America

TABLE OF CONTENTS

AUTHOR'S NOTE

To write my memoir, I consulted my voluminous records and extensive correspondence, including several journals and numerous official and unofficial documents, published interviews and articles and researched old letters. I interviewed several family members and examined family papers and photographs. In what follows I also touch on and share some select pieces of writing from others (with permission or that is in the public domain) that is meaningful to me and helps convey a point or message I want to share with the reader. But reliance on my subjective perceptions of the past is at the heart of this memoir. And my memories of these events and the time it covers in my life.

DEDICATION

This inspirational memoir is dedicated to my parents Frank and Irene Battle Trowell. And also to my siblings, professors and faculty members at several educational institutions: Columbia Hospital School of Nursing, New Jersey City University, Yale University and Teachers College, Columbia University. And to the past, present and future students that I have mentored and will mentor—thank you for rewarding experiences past, present and those yet to come.

ACKNOWLEDGMENTS

This is one of the most difficult parts of my memoir to write since it encompasses my entire life and professional career with family, friends, church, and educational institutions. I wish to express my gratitude to my family and all those who shared their life events and stories for this book to inspire others and pay it forward for future generations.

As with any work of this magnitude, this book is the result of the efforts and collaboration of numerous people in the federal, civilian and military arenas.

At the risk of attempting to list all individuals, I will do so knowing that inadvertently and unintentionally other names may be omitted. However, their assistance was and is just as important. There were so many people who educated me, mentored me and offered me challenging opportunities to excel over the span of my life. I give special thanks to my family members who completed university degrees in medicine, nursing, aviation, health informatics, engineering, business administration, accounting, environmental health, law enforcement and other professional areas. You inspire me every day to see the outcomes of paying it forward for future generations.

After considering for many years that I should write a book and collecting information on and reviewing various publishing companies and ghostwriter services to help me, I decided in August 2009 to write my first book. However, serendipity enabled me to contact an expert ghostwriter and publisher. About that same time in 2009 when I decided to write a book. I read an email message from a flag officer about a company interested in working with general officers to help them write and publish books. After sending an email message to them asking for more information, I immediately received an email back with some information and a draft book-cover image. That is when I first met Dennis Lowery, a superstar and an extraordinary writer and publisher!

I want to thank an important mentor, Major General Paul Weaver, Jr., USAF, (Retired). Not only for his mentoring but also for his confidence in me and for taking the risk of appointing me as commander of the 105th USAF Clinic, Newburgh, New York. That event forever changed my life personally and professionally. It was something never done before and I know he took flak for it, but I think I proved him right! There is a close link between his confidence in me then and my career progression and perseverance in writing my first book and now my memoirs.

I also want to thank Lieutenant General John Conway, USAF (Retired) and Lieutenant General Russell Davis, USAF (Retired) – both were crucial to my career and progress to General Officer rank.

Special appreciation goes to my early mentors and military colleagues throughout my career whom I mentioned by name in my first book. Special thanks to my hero and mentor, Lieutenant Colonel Glen Fraser, USAF (Retired), President of the Major General Irene Trowell-Harris Chapter of Tuskegee Airmen, Inc. in Newburgh, New York. Also, Dr. (Colonel) Andrew Buzzelli, USAF

(Retired) a superb commander, Vice-President for Optometric Education and Founding Dean, Kentucky College of Optometry, University of Pikeville.

I also wish to thank my professors at New Jersey City University, Yale and Columbia for their mentoring and guidance in support of my advanced education.

And special thanks to my colleagues at the Aiken County Historical Museum: Brenda Baratto, Director, Elliott Levy, former Director, and Mary White, VA (Department of Veterans Affairs) staff members, Rev. Dr. James E. Victor, Pastor and colleagues of Mt. Olive Baptist Church especially Vijaya R. Lane and Minister Roderick Lane.

I give praise to my brothers and sisters whom supported me over the years and attended my military and civilian promotions and retirement ceremonies in Washington. They all added value to my life in uniquely different ways. Special recognition to Lafayette and Inez Trowell, who helped take care of our mother by relocating her in their home the last 18 months of her life. They are still role models for youth and community leaders to emulate.

High praise for an uncle, Reverend Jacob C. Trowell, who was always there for the family and is still offering support, advice, and spiritual guidance.

Finally, I could not have written this book without the advice and support of Dennis M. Lowery, President of Adducent, Inc. I was consistently amazed by his advice, creativity, and ability to describe situations with clarity and simplicity. I have great respect and admiration for him, his editors and the supporting staff, led by his oldest daughter Karen Lowery at Adducent and their publishing imprints.

Last, but not least: I apologize to all those who have been with me over the course of the years and whose names I have failed to mention.

INTRODUCTION

"Your whole life comes alive when you have the determination to follow a dream. To create change, to do what is right over what is easy, and have the courage to value tomorrow as much as you do today. I've done this my entire life and know it to be true."

— Dr. Irene Trowell-Harris

It's now more than 55 years since I received my nursing diploma from Columbia Hospital School of Nursing (now the University of South Carolina) in September 1959. There are many other significant educational milestones that followed. You will read about them shortly. But to this day, I have no doubt that my decision to become a nurse—and to continue my education—was the key to my success in life and my leadership career.

This book will focus on sharing my life's journey and the lessons learned along the way. It will include childhood experiences and challenges; how I continue to serve my country by working with veterans who have also served this nation. In it, I also talk about giving back and paying it forward to those who touched my life during a long and exciting journey.

My life and career have both been modeled on and defined by leadership, mentoring, and inspiring others. That's what I focused on in my first book, *Sky High: No Goal is Out of Your Reach*. Written in 2010 as an inspirational tool to inspire others to success; encouraging young people to apply themselves academically and to stay in school and for those stuck-in-place needing a little encouragement to jump-start their careers. This book restates that philosophy but shares a more personal side and a deep personal belief. I believe you will get the sense of what that is throughout as you read. But here is the gist of it: I think attitude determines your quality of existence: what kind of life you've had in the past, how it's going in the present and, most fundamentally, how it will be in your future. Charles Swindoll perfectly describes the significance of attitude in your life:

> "The longer I live, the more I realize the impact of attitude on life. Attitude, to me, is more important than facts. It is more important than the past than education than money than circumstances, than failures, than successes, than what other people think or say or do. It is more important than appearance, giftedness or skill. It will make or break a company... a church... a home. The remarkable thing is we have a choice every day regarding the attitude we will embrace for that day. We cannot change our past... we cannot change the inevitable. The only thing we can do is play on the one string we have, and that is our attitude. I am convinced that life is 10% what happens to me and 90% how I react to it."

At times, we lose control and exhibit a negative attitude. We are human after all. But do yourself a favor, and in your life quickly determine that you will work relentlessly to have a healthy attitude about all things. I'll digress a moment to offer one more bit of advice here, paraphrased from the Bible, James 3:5. It has helped me when it comes to attitude and emotions: *"The tongue is very light (in weight), but few can hold it."* So as control of attitude is important in your life; so is watching what we say when we are emotional, stressed, and under pressure.

There's another lesson I learned that's important to share. So I'll do it with a story that has been around for centuries and is still relevant today:

Once there were two monks on a pilgrimage, an older one who had been on several, and a young monk on his first. One day they came to the edge of a river. It was turbulent, roiling, with several days of rain in the mountains feeding it. It would prove difficult, but not impossible, to cross; they were both solidly built men. They heard crying. Nearby, under a willow tree, a woman sat weeping. In her hands was a small bag she clutched to her chest. She heard them and looked up.

"Please help me... I'm afraid to cross." She gestured at the river and gripped her bag tighter. "But I must get home soon."

The young monk turned his back on her. Their order was forbidden to speak to or touch women. But the older monk picked up the woman and without a word forged the river. He put her down on the other side and with thanks that he didn't respond to; she turned to the right-hand path and hurriedly went on her way.

The older monk continued straight ahead. The younger came after him. They walked in silence for another mile. The young monk, who had been fuming since crossing the river, began berating the older.

"How could you do that — the woman... you've broken your vows." He continued talking to him that way for another mile. Finally, the older monk stopped and turned to him.

"I only carried her across the river — you've been carrying her ever since."

The takeaway from this story is this: Don't carry around more in life than you have to. Learn to set aside anger, and to consider what you say before you say it; learn to control your attitude and develop a good, positive, one. There are so many positive things that come from this that they are too numerous to mention here. But I know from personal experience the benefits they yield if you follow these simple bits of advice.

* * *

In chapter one, I talk about my awakening. And what I tell you seems as if this was a defined period, but it truly has lasted my lifetime. You'll read that it began with the long journey from the farm, country church, and cotton fields, to nursing school, New Jersey City University, Yale, Columbia for progressively higher education. To rising through the ranks and earning 2-stars (Major General) in the United States Air Force and Air National Guard. To having a Tuskegee Airmen chapter named in my honor. To the Brookings Institution leadership seminars. To becoming a White House political appointee serving two presidents as a member of the Senior Executive Service (SES) at the Department of Veterans Affairs. To writing two books.

The Senior Executive Service

The Senior Executive Service (SES) lead America's workforce. As the cornerstone of the Civil Service Reform Act of 1978, the SES was established: "To ensure that the executive management of the Government of the United States is responsive to the needs, policies, and goals of the Nation and otherwise is of the highest quality." These leaders possess well-honed executive skills and share a broad perspective of government and a public service commitment that is grounded in the Constitution. Members of the SES serve in the key positions just below the top presidential appointees. SES members are the major link between these appointees and the rest of the federal workforce. They operate and oversee nearly every government activity in approximately seventy-five federal agencies. The United States Office of Personnel Management (OPM) manages the overall federal executive personnel program, providing the day-to-day oversight and assistance to agencies.

An essential point in my life is that I loved all my job experiences in my career, whether civilian sector, military, federal or political arenas. I made the best of each position, took it on and enhanced job performance and attempted to make system changes for improvement of services.

After leaving the military, I had considered working for a defense contractor or IBM but decided to join the Department of Veterans Affairs. More on this later, but suffice to say my civilian career has been challenging at times, but very rewarding. I had the opportunity to serve as nurse manager, supervisor, chief nurse executive and Flight Nurse Examiner. I've also been a university professor, military commander, Senior Policy Specialist, American Nurses Association (ANA). In government, I've been Director, Northeast Region, Office of Healthcare Inspections, Office of Inspector General, and Director, Center for Women Veterans both at the Department of Veterans Affairs, Washington, DC.

History in Brief - US Department of Veterans Affairs

http://www.va.gov/opa/publications/archives/docs/history_in_brief.pdf

President Reagan signed legislation in 1988 to elevate VA (Department of Veterans Affairs) to Cabinet status and, on March 15, 1989, the Veterans Administration became the Department of Veterans Affairs. Edward J. Derwinski, the VA administrator at the time, was appointed the first Secretary of Veterans Affairs.

As my career progressed; I became disillusioned with attempting to make system changes in health facilities based on the job experience, education and committee work. Then, I decided to change career direction pursuing legislation, advocacy, and political networking. I focused on positions and experience that equipped me with the following:

- Knowledge of the legislative process and health care delivery systems.
- Experience with Joint Commission on Accreditation of Healthcare Organizations and other regulatory agencies.
- Vision and perspective on national oversight of quality assurance and quality improvement including women's health programs, benefits, policies, and legislation.

- Ability to research, prepare, review, and present Congressional testimony.

My long and challenging journey has been supported throughout by strong relationships with many special people that had a great impact on my personally and professionally. I'll mention some of them here.

In the military (ANG/USAF): Maj. Gen. Paul Weaver, Jr., a pilot and Base Commander. As a Flight Chief Nurse: Brig. Gen. Sarah Wells and Brig. Gen. Barbara Goodwin. Lt. Gen. John Conway, Lt. Gen. Russell Davis, and Lt. Col. Beatrice Goodwin.

In my education: Professor James L. Malfetti, Mentor (Columbia University), Dr. Lawrence Michael Wexler, Dissertation Sponsor/Committee Member and Professor John P. Allegrante, Dissertation Committee Member (Columbia University), Professor John D. Thompson, Mentor and Essay Advisor (Yale University), Faculty Advisor, Dr. Rosemary A. Stevens, Associate Professor Public Health/Medical Care (Yale University).

Each taught me something different: leadership, how to handle the media, dealing with politics, handling stress, counseling others on career progression, and how to become a mentor to others. Much of what you'll read in this book is a result of applying what I learned from these wonderful people.

PROLOGUE

"Without a humble but reasonable confidence in your own powers you cannot be successful or happy."

— Norman Vincent Peale

I read a little story not long ago that strengthened my belief that many people yearn for something more IN their life, more TO their life, and must create opportunities for themselves. I'll share it with you here:

THE WATERGIRL by Dennis Lowery

Every morning it was her job to bring water to wash, to mix with meal to make flat bread and to drink. She followed the trail up and over the small ridge that shrouded and protected the home site from an open range scoured by the wind. The path had been created by countless years of bare feet. Her grandmother and mother's before and after her, likely a daughter's; the child she would bear before long. Barely a teen she was of an age for a husband. It would be soon.

It was not what she wished for. The missionary had taught her to read before she died. And the traders had left a few books. Some with pictures of a world and life she could not fathom. Seeing them... reading the words left her changed with a vague feeling of discontent.

It was quiet and cool by the river. There in the still sleeping darkness before the heat of the sun—she felt it already on her back as she descended to the bank— burnt it away. She paused for a moment but couldn't take more time than what was expected. She thought of how the missionary had told her of cities and far lands. Of the world and how large it was. With a sigh she didn't realize had come from her... she stooped to fill her jug.

The sun, higher on the horizon, was on her face as she trudged back to her small existence. All that she knew. In that last cool, peaceful, moment she wondered how other girls, in the so very big world, started their days.

And I can relate to that girl. I've felt the drudgery of the daily ritual, of work in a place I didn't want to be with a hot sun blistering me. Hard manual labor in the cotton fields, day in and day out, is just that; a painful drudgery. And though the opportunity to earn money to help my family was appreciated, those days behind me in the field and the thought of days ahead made me hope for something better in my life. You spend your day sweltering, bending and pulling over and over again. Until even young muscles and joints are tired and aching. I would look up from the work and be thankful for each and any small breath of wind that would bring even a moment's respite.

One day something crossed the bright blue sky, cutting a path beneath that merciless, brutal South Carolina summer sun. I raised my hand to shield my eyes from the light so I could follow it as it left a trail. Blinking the sweat from my eyes, I watched it twinkle, the metal of the airplane's fuselage and wings, until it climbed higher and was out of sight. That moment changed me, changed the course of my life, forever. Like *The Water Girl,* I began to wonder about the world far from where I was—far from the cotton fields.

From that day on I watched for them—those wings in the sky. I thought how wonderful it would be to fly and could only imagine the sensation of being among the clouds, riding on a fresh wind over the summer-baked Earth below. I began to dream that someday I would fly. Someday I would be one of those people flying so high above. I told my family of my dreams and some of them had doubts I would ever make it. It's a very long way from a cotton field to the sky.

But I was fortunate. Unlike *The Water Girl,* I had a mother who had wanted and longed for something to better her position in life. That is a powerful thing; a parent or close loved one that wished for me what they'd been unable to do for themselves. And I was born in a country and time where changes were taking place for minorities to have opportunities though there was still much work to be done and it was not easy. But I took comfort from those who loved me and urged me to follow a dream and work toward my goal and to always believe in what this poem says about the human spirit:

Invictus (by the English poet William Ernest Henley (1849–1903)

Out of the night that covers me,
Black as the pit from pole to pole,
I thank whatever gods may be
For my unconquerable soul.

In the fell clutch of circumstance
I have not winced nor cried aloud.

Under the bludgeoning of chance
My head is bloody but unbowed.

Beyond this place of wrath and tears
Looms but the Horror of the shade,
And yet the menace of the years
Finds and shall find me unafraid.

It matters not how strait the gate,
How charged with punishments the scroll,
I am the master of my fate:
I am the captain of my soul.

PART 1

EARLY LIFE, PROFESSION & CAREER

"A dream is a path of the future, a quiet belief in the heart...

A small, secret wish nurtured deep in the spirit where all great accomplishments start.

A dream is an endless horizon that only the dreamer can see.

A dream is a challenge to all that you are...a promise of all can be!"

— Amanda Bradley

CHAPTER ONE

THE AWAKENING

"It's important to live 'in' the present, but we must live 'for' tomorrow. The present lasts for only one second... one minute... one hour... one day. The future stretches before us to infinity. What are you doing in the present to create a better tomorrow?"

— Dennis Lowery

I was born toward the end of the Great Depression in September of 1939. My parents, Irene Battle Trowell and Frank Trowell had only a third-grade education but were wise in what they wanted for their children. I'm the third of eleven children (I have three sisters and seven brothers). I did not remember the Depression era. However, my uncle Reverend Jacob Calvin Trowell, a World War II veteran, college graduate and minister told me about his experiences. About the government trucks stopping near our home in Montmorenci, South Carolina delivering flour, powdered milk, and peanut butter to farmers. From them, I learned truly how hard things had been, in that time when I was too young to realize it. I also learned that even when you don't have much—you must appreciate what you do have. My parents taught me and my siblings strong family values, a commitment to excellence in work ethic and a good religious foundation. They taught us discipline and helped us structure our lives and careers. Our mother especially, and consistently, stressed the value of getting a good education. The things they taught me have been the bedrock of every success in my life.

My brothers, sisters and I grew up and worked on that small cotton farm. We also raised chickens, pigs, cows, turkeys, corn, peas, watermelons and assorted vegetables in the garden. When needed, we would barter with other families and neighbors for different types of fruits and vegetables. We used kerosene lamps for light, a wood heater for heating the house and a wood stove for cooking. We boiled our clothes in a pot with homemade lye soap (trust me you never want to get that in your eyes). We bathed in a tin tub with well water pumped by hand, though later on we had an electric pump. Our toilet was an outhouse. When we completed work on our parent's farm, we would help other people with their farms by chopping cotton for $3.00 per day or pulling corn fodder for the mules. My older sister and I worked in restaurants after school to purchase our first black and white TV and to build an indoor bathroom. My mother made most of our clothing using a sewing machine. At times, we shared clothing as hand-me-downs from older siblings. Early on, we used a mule and wagon for transportation since we did not own a car.

My awakening was a long journey from that cotton field in the 1950s where I discovered a vision and my dream. I grew up with an insatiable desire to learn and to look at life differently. That conflicted with what society expected of women, and especially of minority women, at that time. Women were supposed to marry a local boy and have many children to take care of house and home and to work on the farm. I thought differently and decided I wanted to attend college and travel before getting married and having a family.

I believe the way my mother approached life was an important lesson and philosophy that she bestowed on her children. She wanted more in her own life, but circumstances prevented it. That did not stop her from teaching us that there was a better world out there, and to pursue opportunities to get there as early as possible in life. And to not let a life we never wanted harden around us and become the life that we had to live. She encouraged us to have dreams and faith that we could achieve them.

That willingness to go after what I wanted formed a lifelong attitude and philosophy that has served me well. And her simple words, simple—yet powerful—wisdom, helped her and my father raise eleven children of their own and seventeen foster children. Following those words enabled many of them to have successful careers in medicine, aviation, nursing, law enforcement, small business and the military. I'm a perfect example of how following my mother's advice led to a career of accomplishment that I never imagined as a child and young woman. For young people—following those simple words can help you too!

As a family, we attended services at Mount Hill Missionary Baptist Church on Sundays, first for Sunday school then the regular service that lasted the rest of the day on occasions. As a family, we also ate together for breakfast and supper every day. There was a prayer of thanks before each meal. On Sunday morning, we had a special breakfast of homemade rolls, grits, bacon, and cheese with eggs. That was a wonderful family treat. The challenge for my siblings and I was attempting to catch-up on school assignments and studies. Many children had difficulty catching up after missing so many days of school while working on the farm. As the children reached the 10th grade in high school, in addition to farm work, we got jobs in local fast food restaurants to supplement the family income.

Another challenge for my siblings was helping to take care of our brother who was born with cerebral palsy and was not able to walk or talk. We all took care of him until he died at 32 years of age. In spite of the hard work and school challenges, we were happy. Maybe we were not aware of the material things we lacked that signified the American dream or privileges other people enjoyed. With this—I often wonder why some people with fame, wealth, opportunities and almost everything a person could want, commit suicide or abuse alcohol or drugs. Why do some people that appear to have everything seem so unhappy? I don't think we ever really know the answer or answers to that, but we were always grateful for small things and minor accomplishments.

During that time in the South, black families worked on the farm and children only attended school once the crops were completely harvested, usually starting in October rather than August when school started. I attended a segregated one-room school, Oakwood Elementary (now known as Cushman Academy) in Aiken from first to eighth grade. My teachers Mrs. Hazel J. Cadle and Mrs. Alberta Scott taught all eight grades for a salary of $90.00 a month. I graduated in May 1952 and attended Martha Schofield High School for grades nine through twelve graduating as an honor student in June 1956. I was May Day Beauty Queen and served as class president in 11th grade. Other activities I was involved in included photo club, canteen assistant, hall patrol, NHA club and a class officer. Also, I was voted as one of the best-dressed senior students for 1956.

Sad to say, but not uncommon at the time, I was not encouraged to attend college by most of my teachers. Some teachers assumed, if you were low-income if your parents were not professionals and if you were from a large family, that there was no opportunity for college. That type of thinking, unfortunately, ruled out encouraging students to find alternative ways to find money for college. It was as if your life was set on a concrete path that could not deviate.

I wanted something different than what other people thought was my lot in life. I found, through planning and then working, to follow the plan that you can do much in life that others may think can't be accomplished.

Since I was an honor student, I consulted with my homeroom teacher and the principal about my plans for after high school. They took an interest but waited until I was admitted to the nursing school and could present one semester of grades. After that, I received an annual scholarship. Opportunities generally come to you once you've proved yourself.

One teacher stands out. I had great respect for my homeroom teacher, Mrs. Lelia A. Bradby, a graduate of Hampton Institute and Cornell University with majors in English and French. She was very intelligent and had traveled extensively around the world. She wanted her students to succeed but had misgivings because she saw so many poor children who would never find it within themselves to break free of poverty's stranglehold. She saw how serious I was, and that I was committed to doing what was necessary. To study as hard and as much as I could and to work toward a goal. She always made time to talk with me about my hopes, dreams, and plans. She gave me good advice and continued to mentor me even through nursing school. After completing high school, I visited at intervals and received an invitation to speak to the student body after graduating from nursing school. Even then, I felt the responsibility to share with others what I had done. With the hope that they would see that they could follow their dreams too—even if it takes many small steps to get there instead of one large jump.

I knew that I had to focus on what I wanted and never lose sight of what I had envisioned for myself.

> *"...the location of the body is much less important than the location of the mind, and the former has*

surprisingly little influence on the latter. The heart goes where the head takes it, and neither cares much about the whereabouts of the feet."
— John Tierney, New York Times

Everything. All that we are and that we become. Everything starts with how you think and what you believe. And that doesn't matter where you are. Even in a cotton field in the late 1950s South Carolina. How focused your thinking is... is tied to how happy you are. I think you must generate a fair share of focused thought to have a meaningful life and that is what makes you happy.

To achieve it, we don't all have to be geniuses or philosophers, with our time mostly spent in concentrated thought or contemplation on world matters. Or in pondering the rightness or wrongness of human actions at any given time. But to make our own lives better (and those around us) takes concentration on those things that are important to us (and to them). Daydreaming, idle speculation and stream-of-consciousness thinking are fine and everyone has those moments during the day. But consider this:

"Life is not long," Samuel Johnson said, *"and too much of it must not pass in idle deliberation how it shall be spent."*

I know I'm always happiest when focusing on something. When I have something definite I'm trying to create, finish or give complete attention to—that's when I feel most alive. At a personal level, it could be in special moments with family, travel or exercise. At a professional level, I also get that same sense of satisfaction when working to improve organizations and mentoring individuals.

This works the same if we are unhappy with present circumstances. Focus on finding solutions. Don't complain or wallow in self-pity or cower in fear... think of alternatives... come up with a plan... seek out help. Take action, but don't act mindlessly. Think and then do. Even small steps are incremental progress. And that sense of doing something good, accomplishing a goal no matter big or small... the feeling of progress at many different levels in life is something we should all desire and strive for.

I believe that is where the heart and mind become one. And they can happen no matter where we live or where we are... we carry within us the very things that can create happiness for us.

I wasn't happy with my present circumstances. But even with the back-breaking work in the fields early in my life, I was, and still am, appreciative that we had the opportunity to pick cotton since this was a paying job. And that was how our family survived. In our area, in the 1960s and 1970s the mechanized cotton picker began to replace people. That machine reduced harvest time and maximized efficiency. It played an indispensable role in the transition from the pre-World War II South of over-population, sharecropping, and hand labor to the capital-intensive agriculture of the new South. The Rust Picker could do the work of between 50 and 100 hand pickers. This is how Donald Holley, from the University of Arkansas at Monticello, described the history of the progression from handpicked to the mechanical cotton picker.

> *"Until the Second World War, the Cotton South remained poor, backward, and unmechanized. With minor exceptions, most tasks — plowing, cultivating, and finally harvesting cotton — were done by hand. Though sharecropping stifled the region's attempts to mechanize, too many farmers, both tenants, and owners, were trying to survive on small,*

uneconomical farms, trapping themselves in poverty. From 1910 to 1970 the Great Migration, which included whites as well as blacks, reduced the region's oversupply of small farmers and embodied a tremendous success story for both migrants and the region itself. The mechanical cotton picker played an indispensable role in the transition from the prewar South of over-population, sharecropping, and hand labor to the capital-intensive agriculture of the postwar South."

On my recent visit in February 2015 to Aiken, South Carolina, driving from Augusta Bush Field Airport to Aiken, I observed a beautiful cotton field with a mechanized cotton picker parked near Highway 215. It vividly reminded me of memories from decades ago picking and harvesting cotton.

Cotton Field, Salley, SC, 2014

There were not many career opportunities for minority women in 1956. The best were becoming a teacher, secretary or nurse. I valued my teachers in school and what they instilled in me, but one of the choices appealed more strongly to me.

I decided to become a nurse, something my mother had desired for herself. She knew nurses were always in demand and it was a path to making more money for her family. But was unable to attend school because what she earned from working went to help her parents survive financially—nothing was left to go toward nursing school. She was trapped in that vicious cycle of having to work and it takes all you earn for your family to survive; never able to have the extra money or time to improve yourself. But still my mother always dreamed of becoming a nurse. Her dreams were realized when my sister Mae, and I became nurses.

My mother's desire to go to nursing school made an impact on me, but I was also influenced by meeting a nurse at our family doctor's medical office. At family visits, she was interested in how I was doing in school and would always talk to me. She really cared that I was doing well and wanted to know about my plans for after high school. She would talk to me about what she thought about being a nurse, and gave me brochures for different nursing schools so I could learn more about that as something to consider for after graduation. She believed that I would do well as a nurse. Her steady voice of support and confidence meant a lot and gave me an even stronger sense of determination to prove she was right about me.

Aside from the practical and economic attractiveness of nursing, a most compelling reason was the desire to care for and help others—a trait instilled in me by my mother and father. I felt then and still do now that my desire to become a nurse was a divine calling to help others and not just a means to further my own interests. Nurses often consider their profession a calling. Florence

Nightingale, the founder of modern nursing, characterized her spiritual motivation to serve others as an "inward tug."

My brothers, sisters and I were raised with a belief that we all have a responsibility to help those in need and to contribute in any way we could. As I mentioned one of my brothers was born with cerebral palsy, was blind and unable to speak and our family members cared for him for 32 years until his death in 1969. I saw the importance of being a caregiver firsthand and that having a trained nurse in the family would have helped early on. My desire was to attend A&T University in North Carolina, a four-year nursing university, but I did not have the initial $1,000 needed for tuition.

My parents didn't have much and what money I earned working in high school went to help them and pay for things I and my siblings needed. We just didn't have extra for college. One Sunday, I mentioned to a church elder that I wanted to go to nursing school. I talked to her about my high school grades and accomplishments to show I was eligible to get in and had been accepted. But I needed financial help. She told me that she would speak to the minister and see what could be done.

The next Sunday she came up to me and said that she had talked to the minister and needed to speak to my mother, too. After the service, she told us that they were going to take up a collection for me to make my first tuition payment at nursing school. My mother thanked her and I was so excited. After the service, they passed around a wicker plate, more of a basket, and people dropped in nickels, dimes, and quarters. Folks in my community didn't have a lot of money. So in that basket there weren't any paper bills, but it was full of coins. By the time it had made it up and down the pews, when we counted out, it came to $61.25 (I needed $60.00). So that was my first tuition payment. The church provided the bridge I needed to get from the cotton field to the nursing school. My high school, Martha Schofield, offered a scholarship for my remaining two years of nursing school.

Now, I had to leave home. And I never had before, not even for a single night. But now I was going to strange place with a lot of responsibilities to not let down those who helped get me there. All I could think was that it was great; I don't ever want to come back to a cotton field. I remembered that terribly hot day in the field a few years before when I looked up to watch an airplane in the sky... and dream. This collection my church gave me was the first bridge to reach my goals.

The last Sunday before I left for nursing school in Columbia, at dinner, my mother told how proud she was of me. I was about to become a nurse and that was something she always wanted for herself but never able to do. She told me, "This is my gift to you— pick up your plate..." I did and under it was a $50.00 bill. I was amazed and touched. I'm sure it was all the money she had at the time and it was the single largest amount of money I had seen in one bill. "It'll help you at school." My mother smiled and hugged me. It was a wonderful dinner with my family that I will always remember vividly. That evening I left for Columbia. I had to start school the next morning.

In high school, my sister Frances and I had also both been employed at fast food restaurants to pay for school related expenses and supplement the family income. We purchased our first black and white TV and helped install indoor plumbing. When we had enough money saved, we bought a 1956 Crown Victoria Ford to drive to school and to work afterward. The car was sky blue and white with a crown across the top and on both sides of the car. It was the sharpest car in our high school parking lot. All the boys really loved it! My sister had moved to New York to work so the car was mine. I hadn't driven very much and was somewhere between home in Aiken and Columbia when I had a flat tire. Now, I had never had to change a flat but I had seen my father and brothers change one. I knew no one was going to stop and help me. I got out the jack and lug wrench; jacked up the car and got the flat off and put the spare on and was on my way.

At that young age, I knew the importance of family but I was also starting to realize the importance of community. They gave what they could to help me and that little bit of money (now... for them it was a lot back then) made all the difference in my world and in my life. But it wouldn't have happened if I hadn't simply told the church elder my dream of going to nursing school and asked for help. And I think the reason they did help me was because I showed the qualities and capabilities to succeed. So I've learned in life it is imperative to ask for help when you need it but also it's equally important that you deserve it. No matter what the question might be... the answer that you're looking will never be known if you don't ask. I believe in Scripture Matthew 7:7 there's a saying that's proven to be true throughout my life.

"Ask and it will be given to you; seek and you will find; knock and the door will be opened to you."

I kept that in mind as I struggled with changing my first flat that evening on the side of a country road. I'd been given an exciting opportunity and wasn't going to fret or complain over a flat tire.

* * *

My first year of nursing school was a cultural shock since that was my first experience away from home. However, I was ecstatic about being admitted to the nursing school and having the opportunity to learn a practical and valuable skill and to use it to help other people. At school, I was paired with a student from Athens, Georgia. Ours was a twin bedroom with a shared bathroom. We enjoyed each other's company, studied together and went to school and social activities. I immediately bonded with my 38 classmates and was excited about their stories and family history. We all enjoyed the hospital type food and even had a different menu selection each day. During my first year, there was very little free time since I was extremely busy getting oriented to a new city, studying, networking with classmates, and working on hospital wards taking care of patients. During that time, I was also seeking a local church to attend and worship. I received several recommendations of various churches, visited most to check out the services and eventually selected one which became an extended family to me.

***

I know that who I am deep inside is what has carried me through the good and bad of life: triumphs and disasters... births and deaths... the gamut of human experience. It enabled me to better appreciate all that is good and fine I've experienced in life and to endure pain and tragedy. What I learned from it is the importance of how I feel about myself and who I am. Not a perfect woman or human by any means... but a pretty good person, a very good friend and, I think, an excellent nurse and human being. My personal culture works for me at all times... it makes me who I am.

> *"Why do you and I need a personal culture? Because a culture supports us and empowers us. When we're down, it holds us up. A culture is different from a brand. A brand can be false; it can be constructed artificially to monetize our work or to hype our ego and our narcissism. (A brand, it should be said, can also be real. That's the best kind.) A personal culture is true, whether we're selling something or not. Our*

culture works in a crowd and it works when we're alone; it works at the North Pole or in outer space."
                    −Steven Pressfield, best-selling author

That so many did not make it reinforced how, if you want to succeed in anything, you have to believe and you have to take control of the things that you can. That reminds me of this little story:

The Girl Who Finally Believed in Herself

A very good friend of mine was feeling down and asked for a story... something to make her feel like things would get better. Here is what I told her:

I believe that despite the issues or circumstances, you can take control over your life. And I believe you can control your feelings... and that the belief, though it may come hard at first, does become self-fulfilling. That's what the girl in the story I'll tell you about discovered.

You see, she felt nothing would get better in her life. So many things were wrong she'd never be able to fix them. One autumn day she sat in the park with her closest companion. He scampered and played... chasing this and that and leaves in the wind. But he always returned to her.

Seeing how sad she was, he did something he had never done. He spoke to her. But not aloud... not in a voice like humans. But in the language of the heart. He looked up at her; deep into her eyes and poured all his love... all that he knew about the beautiful world he lived in and the wonderful person he was with.

"It will be okay... if you make it that way... you have to chase and catch the things you want in life. The love and the fun... the person to do that with; the person to be with is out there. They will find you... you will find them... when you start taking control. When you start believing, you can do for yourself what you want most deep in your heart and soul."

He licked her hand and nuzzled her fingers. She was such a good person... all she needed to do was to believe and work each moment of every day to do what she needed to do to create a happy life. It wouldn't be easy he knew. He looked up and smiled.

"But I know you can do it."

And it was hard... but she listened and believed... and she lived happily ever after.

I told her I hoped she held this little story in her heart, each and every day. And it's okay to cry happy tears over it and... to believe... that's where everything in life starts. Everything.

Belief & Faith (in yourself and from others)

While at nursing school, I met Juanita and Andrew Martin, who became my adopted parents in Columbia, South Carolina. Juanita was a licensed practical nurse on the medical-surgical unit at Columbia Hospital and Andrew was a mail carrier. They entertained students with a warm family environment, unconditional love, great home cooked meals, barbecues, television and birthday parties. When we felt overwhelmed by the academic rigor of nursing school and being away from home, they believed in and comforted us just like our parents.

Juanita and Andrew Martin celebrated their 50th wedding anniversary on June 2, 2001, which I attended with other Columbia Hospital graduates. I gave them a Waterford crystal United States Capitol Dome and a plaque making them honorary parents for their unconditional love, inspiration and mentoring. We have kept in touch with each other since 1956 remaining close even after more than five decades. Unfortunately, we lost Andrew in December 2009 but I am still in contact with Juanita.

* * *

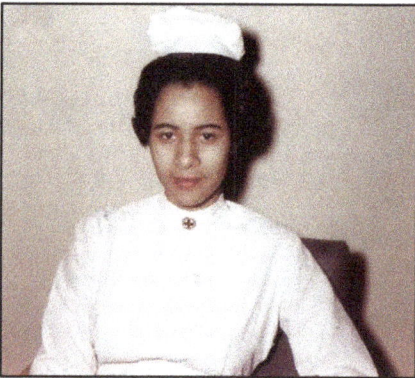

Nursing School Graduation Uniform September 1959

Nurses have a tremendous responsibility when caring for patients and supporting their family members. Nurses are there at the beginning and the end, birth, and death, and all of life between these events.

They use their specialized knowledge, experience, and skills to initiate life-saving measures, improve and promote the health and well-being of patients, and ease pain, suffering, and loss. We (nurses) are all united in that common mission—regardless of where we work: in the military, federal or civilian arenas. And so it does not matter the nurse's position title, or whether employed, unemployed or self-employed.

During my career, I worked to raise the standards of my own practice and my profession as a whole, mainly addressing system and policy initiatives. Nursing is my life's work and I have worked in various areas: as a civilian and military nurse, and nursing/medical/health care related executive at the federal level. However, regardless of what title I had at any given time, and whether directly or indirectly working with consumers of healthcare I always have been a nurse. It is who I am. In each role, I embraced the same mission of consistent ideals and ethical and practice standards and responsibility as a health care provider.

What type of traits help make nurses successful? There are many examples of them in nursing literature; however, I like the list from the Pulse Uniform Health Care Update of 10 Traits:

1. Empathy
2. Compassion
3. Patience
4. Diligence
5. Genuine Interest
6. Good Communication
7. Diplomacy
8. Motivation
9. Balanced View of Profession and Personal Career
10. A Positive View of Life.

Positive character traits are those things that draw us to other people. When someone is generous, kind, energetic, or optimistic, they exude an energy that attracts others. People that exude them typically perform at high levels in their profession and career.

CHAPTER TWO

BUILDING A BRIDGE OVER THE UNKNOWN

"For what it's worth... it's never too late, or in my case too early, to be whatever you want to be. There's no time limit. Start whenever you want. You can change or stay the same. There are no rules for this thing. We can make the best or the worst of it. I hope you make the best of it. I hope you see things that startle you. I hope you feel things you never felt before. I hope you meet people who have a different point of view. I hope you live a life you're proud of, and if you're not, I hope you have the courage to start all over again."

— F. Scott Fitzgerald

I believe that family—not self—come first. There is a balance that you need in life but if you are able to help, then you should. The extra money and ability to help my family gave me a sense of empowerment and knowledge that I could and did make a difference not only in my life but also in the life of others. There is something about that feeling that is both sobering and frees your thinking. You are no longer bound by considerations of just yourself. Your mind is opened up and presented a much bigger picture of the world around you. It's not that you are responsible for the well-being of that world or that you have to try to do everything for everyone. It is not that at all. It is simply that you understand even with the small things and a limited number of people that perhaps you can only affect. If you do in a positive way, they in turn might influence others similarly or go on to do good or even great things. All because in some small way you helped them or were a positive influence. The ripples from that can travel thousands of miles, spread throughout the years and create that truest, purest most wholesome legacy that anyone could ever hope for. I was proud to be a registered nurse in that starched white uniform and cap ready to help others, including my family. To help comfort another person made me feel wonderful. Whether it was giving them something to help relieve their pain or other medications, bathing, feeding, helping them to walk, giving a back rub for comfort. Even just spending time listening (really listening) to the patient's concerns. That is how it is when your work is not just work... it's something more than just a vocation. It's part of your identity.

* * *

"Only those who play win. Only those who risk win. History favors risk-takers. Forgets the timid. Everything else is commentary."

— Iveta Cherneva

I immediately found many nursing positions and an opportunity to return to school for a graduate degree. On completing the psychiatric nursing course, I accepted a position at New York Hospital in New York City with super benefits and an excellent salary. I relocated to New York City and lived in the New York Hospital housing. This was another milestone in my life—touring famous sites, I'd only read, heard about, or seen in movies. I went to jazz concerts, shopped in Manhattan, went to shows at Radio City Music Hall, operas, and plays and ate at some of the fantastic restaurants. I loved the hustle and bustle of the stock market—it was busy but also had an organization to it... a pattern to the way it worked that I got a tremendous charge from when I visited. In New York, I felt like a plant must feel when it is finally watered, freshens and blossoms. I truly knew I was at the world's doorstep and had just been invited in. It was a fabulous experience, which I thoroughly enjoyed. I had many family members and friends always visiting me when I lived there and I became an expert tour guide.

At the hospital, there were bright and energetic medical and nursing students eager to learn. I had the opportunity to work with them and their faculty members. I was a staff nurse, quickly moved up to an assistant, and then head nurse. That sounds great and may seem that things just fell into place for me, but it wasn't quite that simple. I believe firmly that a strong work ethic and interest in furthering yourself does more for your chances of success than any amount of passive wishing and dreaming.

Nursing School Graduation Uniform with Cape Sept. 1959

I worked all the hours I could, which not only made me more money but also accelerated my level of experience. I learned more and faster by doing extra work and reaching for new things to learn and do. I approached everything I did then and still do now with the basic common sense to do my job responsibly, to be on time and never shirk. And when new opportunities came from that, as they will if you have that attitude, I took them on with a willingness to try as hard as I could and not accept mediocrity.

After one year at the hospital something happened that changed my life forever.

It all started with a chance conversation with two nurses I did not know while working at New York Hospital. We were walking down the corridor toward the cafeteria and I overheard them mention being on flight status. Curious, I asked them what they meant.

They told me they were in the New York Air National Guard. This was in the early years of the Vietnam War, and flight nurses were badly needed. When they told me about what a Flight Nurse did and where they worked, my dream of flying awakened and over our break and afterward I asked them several questions about the National Guard requirements and commitment. They eagerly filled me in and asked if I wanted to go with them the next drill weekend to Floyd Bennett Field and learn more. I wanted to know about the negatives as well as the benefits and agreed to go with them, but I couldn't that month and did the next.

That drill weekend I talked with other flight nurses, pilots and engineers, who were happy to take the time to answer my questions. I spoke longest with a Tech Sergeant in personnel.

He told me he had joined after high school and had been in for 18 years. He told me about all the training schools and that it was the military and not like the civilian world I had only known to that point in my life. Joining the Air National Guard meant duty one weekend per month and in any time of emergency, war or natural catastrophe, I would likely be called to active duty. It was a commitment that I needed to think about.

After that weekend, I thought seriously about it for the next two months. It was a big decision—and life-changing one—but one I knew I had to make. It was an opportunity to fulfill my dreams.

I thought it was destiny: for me to ask my church to help, to receive it, to attend and then complete nursing school. To move even farther away from the South where I'd been born and raised to work in New York City. Where I would meet two nurses, I did not know who would tell me about opportunities in the Air National Guard. If I took this opportunity... it would mean I would fly. I couldn't ignore all of that and decided to join.

Once I did I had to arrange time off from my job for basic orientation training and then six weeks of Flight Nurse school. I went to a two-week basic orientation school in Alabama. I also got to make an orientation flight, only two hours, on a C-97 Stratofreighter, a four-engine propeller aircraft. That was the type of aircraft I would expect to be frequently flying on in the NYANG (New York Air National Guard).

C-97 Stratofreighter

We took off from Floyd Bennett Field in Brooklyn. On the two-hour flight, they showed us all the position responsibilities and we talked with the flight crew: the pilot, co-pilot, and engineer, about what they did in flight. I was fascinated as the crew told us about flight physics and physiology.

When I told my mother I was joining the Air National Guard she was worried and said, "Those airplanes can crash…" She fretted and was concerned for me. But I had absolutely no fear. I felt so comfortable—not scared, not nervous—I felt like my dream had come true. I felt truly alive. That feeling of your plane taking off, climbing and banking, the occasional turbulence and sensation of descending, dropping slowly and the ground coming up to land and then rolling to a stop. It was beyond what I had imagined as a young girl, ten years before, sweat stinging my eyes, as I watched planes fly high overhead. On the flight, I looked down and wondered if some little boy or girl was looking up at the silver wings in the sky and dreamed of flying one day. How I felt at that moment is hard to describe. I think it was a combination of appreciation for those who helped me to get there and pride at the work I had done. And the decisions I had made that led to where I was at that point.

I got my slot for Flight Nurse school, which would begin about six months later. When it was time to report, I drove to San Antonio, Texas with a friend I had met who was also going to the class. In school, I stayed focused on graduating. The cost of my training came to about $50,000 and I wasn't going to waste that investment in me. I couldn't fail all who had helped me get to this point. Some of my like-minded classmates and I formed a study group that helped. Again, I was learning the strength of a community. Flight school was not just training in medical practices and processes. It was also on how to respond and perform them under extreme stress. A lack of sleep and adverse conditions were part of what we had to contend with. Situations like simulating a plane crash at night in the woods. Performing triage and deciding who had a chance to survive and which of the hurt and wounded didn't; dealing with catastrophic injuries, severed limbs all the while having to make decisions without emotion. Because if you became emotional it could result in making a wrong decision and someone possibly dying. It was a tremendous responsibility.

The academics I could handle. The stress and pressure were something I learned to control. Back then, there was still a feeling, a subtle prejudice, that we (me and the other minority student in the class) were watched closer than the other nurses in the class. I did get the sense that some instructors felt minorities didn't deal well with flying. I am not responsible for what people think or what they believe. I am responsible for what I think, say and do in my life. Everyone has responsibility for themselves to decide what their own reality and perception of who they are as an individual; their sense of self-worth.

At school, and in the air, it all felt natural. Yet, it was so different than anything I had experienced—a total unknown. But then my personal faith and confidence in my abilities and my spiritual faith, made me feel sure in what I was doing and that I belonged. I graduated near the top of my class.

I had never forgotten that moment in the cotton field, watching the airplane cut a swath through the sky—far and away from toiling in the hot fields. From that day, it seemed everything I'd done, planned and worked toward, had led me to where I was at that point in time. The right place and time to meet two people I never would have met otherwise. I still keep in touch with one of them. Our friendship, over the years, along with many others equally as long, shows that the continuity and consistency of relations are crucial to your quality of life. That plays a role in anchoring you in a way that a more transient relationship style might never accomplish.

That visit to the airfield significantly affected the rest of my life. Talking with my two new friends about their experience and a chance conversation with a Tech Sergeant, who shared with me his thoughts on how his service in the Air National Guard benefited him. Helped me make the decision to join the New York Air National Guard. That decision led me to become a commissioned officer and enter Flight Nurse training and to seek an Air Force career and pursue a graduate degree.

* * *

You can feel the transition moment when a jet has kicked in the afterburners or as a pilot; you push forward on the throttles and feel the vibration and surge. When I made the decision to join the Air National Guard and to pursue becoming a Flight Nurse, I felt the same way. I had now entered another new world and stage in my life. From this point on, my civilian and military careers paralleled—each would be marked and milestones reached with a steady progression of new positions, advancing education, new responsibilities, and new rewards. I steadily extended the bridge I had built so far to the life I enjoy today. A few months after receiving my Flight Nurse wings in 1964, I was onboard a C-97, that crashed while landing in Charleston, South Carolina. Though onboard the aircraft, I learned the exact details after the accident was investigated and written up. This was my first cross-country flight after completing Flight Nurse school.

We left Floyd Bennett Field in Brooklyn, New York on a Friday evening traveling to San Juan, Puerto Rico with a stop at Charleston AFB, SC to pick up passengers. The weather was clear with no clouds as we headed to South Carolina. There were nineteen people on the airplane, two women and seventeen men; however, the Charleston, SC newspaper described the crash of an Air National Guard airplane with nineteen men onboard. Even though we all were shaken and were very happy to be alive. My parents lived just over 120 miles from Charleston yet read about the crash in the newspaper. But they were not aware that I was involved in the accident.

I was thinking to myself I really did not intend to spend time and energy earning silver wings just to be killed and get them bloody. But that incident did make me think and consider my own planning differently. Even though I had very few material things, I had a car and life insurance. I quickly consulted legal advice and also completed a will. At that point, I surmised that I was saved from death for a reason. I must complete my mission even though I did not have a clue yet what that divine assignment was.

* * *

I remained on flying status accumulating hundreds of hours over nearly twelve years as a Flight Nurse, Flight Nurse Instructor and Flight Nurse Examiner traveling all over the world. Through hard work and determination, I advanced quickly through the ranks, earning promotion to Flight Nurse Instructor in 1966, Flight Nurse Examiner in 1968 and to chief nurse a few years later. It appeared that with my choice to become a nurse and then join the Air National Guard—in spite of different challenges and barriers—life offered me many great opportunities. It seems that I constantly was at the right place at the right time. But in reality, it took me many years of experience to progress in my career and to work toward and receive advanced college degrees. I was always willing to work for what I wanted. I did not have a sense of entitlement nor a need for instant gratification. I knew that as long as I broke down into manageable chunks what I needed to do, that one step at a time, I could get to wherever I decided I needed to go. Again, I built my bridge as I went.

General Officer Orientation (Brigadier General), T-1 Aircraft,
Brooks AFB, San Antonio, TX, March 20 to April 1, 1994

In October 1993, almost 30 years after earning my wings, I received my first star. I was selected to become the first female African-American General Officer in the then 357-year history of the National Guard, the oldest branch of our Armed Forces.

In September 1998, I was promoted to two-star rank, Major General. I retired with that rank on September 29, 2001, after serving in the United States Air Force and Air National Guard for 38 years, 5 months, 26 days and 3 hours. Over that 38-year period, I had the opportunity to serve my country in many capacities.

All the while, I never stopped learning, graduating cum laude with a bachelor's degree from New Jersey City University in 1971. I earned a master's degree in Public Health from Yale University in

1973 and second masters' and a doctorate in health education from Columbia University in 1983.

CHAPTER THREE

SPANNING A LIFE AND LESSONS LEARNED

"The only way that we can live is if we grow. The only way that we can grow is if we change. The only way that we can change is if we learn. The only way we can learn is if we are exposed. And the only way that we can become exposed is if we throw ourselves out into the open. Do it. Throw yourself."

— C. JoyBell C.

Though inspired by my mother and a nurse in our family medical doctor's office to become a nurse my most compelling reason was the desire to care for and help others. Nursing is a wonderful profession. Think about the convenience and benefits of being employed in the profession. Nurses are employed and work in hospitals, clinics, universities, corporations, pharmacies, doctor's offices, department stores, prisons, schools and in numerous other locations. There are also numerous specialty areas including military bases, aircraft and ships, Congress and the White House. Nurses can work various shifts and time-periods including days, evenings, nights, weekends, full-time, part-time, per diem, and private duty. All options with flexibility are conducive to attending college and caring for a family especially those with children.

My life story is not just about me. It is about family, church, community and those that helped me to become successful. Life is like an orchestra; it takes the conductor's direction, skilled musicians, and instruments to produce great music. My story is about a nurse; however, the value of all that helped me over my long life applies to other professions, too.

Some Advice:

To those reading this book; think about where you are today, where you would like to be tomorrow, next week, next month... a year from now... five and ten years from now. What plans have you have made to reach your dream goals? If you are a veteran, a student, a teacher or faculty member, a government worker or employee in small or large businesses or anyone considering retirement. Whether that's far off or uncomfortably close... you may need to reshape or rebuild some of the life and careers you've created based on past choices.

I suggest that you take stock and make a list of your education, experience, and accomplishments. Someone or an institution representative may be looking for what you can offer. If you lack certain things or have weak aspects in those areas, you should consider creating or strengthening them. Opportunities that you did not dream off within your professional career are out there, but they only come through for those who are prepared to take advantage and act on them.

And, of course, we don't always meet with acceptance. Sometimes when we are trying to accomplish something we often worry, "What if I fail... what if I'm rejected?"

"If you're trying to achieve, there will be roadblocks. I've had them; everybody has had them. But obstacles don't have to stop you. If you run into a wall, don't turn around and give up. Figure out how to climb it, go through it, or work around it."
— Michael Jordan

That basic human fear applies to virtually everything we do in life. Most people experience it to a larger or lesser degree. A fragile psyche asks that question over and over again and beating that ball around in your head has to suck. If you have that bouncing around in your head—you must stop it. That is if you want to make progress in many aspects of your life. It could be your profession or relationships, etc., anything under the sun—and moon—that opens you up to someone else's perception or judgment of you. The way to overcome the fear of rejection is to stand up to it. Put yourself out there and be willing to be rejected or to fail... and then learn from experience. Rejection (and failure) is permanent only if you let it become so. No one on this Earth is perfect. Be willing to discover that about yourself—and to discover it in others. Even when you try your best, sometimes you will bomb. It's OK to be concerned about the outcome... just don't let that stop you from trying. Another author I know, Donna McAleer, often quotes this (and it is an absolute truth):

You miss 100% of the shots you don't take.

So...

-- TAKE YOUR SHOT(S)! --

Isn't what you want to accomplish for yourself (or your family if applicable) worth it? That being said you also have to understand this about failure.

> *"There's a lot of emphasis on trying to accelerate the path to success by spending a ton of time studying the methods of those have succeeded before us. In the hope that we'll be able to avoid many of the mistakes they made. And, there is a certain logic to that. But, what it doesn't take into account is the fact that the thing that led them to be able to do what they do is that they, themselves, messed up, over and over and over. And it was that repeated intimate relationship*

with the mistakes that led to a deep enough understanding of why it needed to be done differently that led to their success." From *Make More Bad Stuff* by Jonathan Fields.

I know from personal experience that what Jonathan Fields says is true. You learn the most by being willing to fail. The thing is that most people look at the unknown or something new—especially something creative—and fear rejection. They fear failure. They worry that what turns out won't be what they hope for. So they put it off, they wait for the right time or worse yet they never do it. They never give it a shot. And that's tragic.

All in life is a process of refinement and adjustment. My personal philosophy is that you have to be willing to fail and to deal with it if that is the outcome and keep moving forward to achieve the things you dream of. This book is about my journey over more than six decades. Over the span of my life, there have been many barriers, failures, and disappointments. However, I decided not to allow my life and work be defined by them. I did not let them deny me what I wanted to achieve in my life. Instead, I focused on the successes and even though painful at times, I used my failures as an opportunity to grow. In spite of challenges: I was able to earn Flight Nurse wings, become a United States Air Force, Major General, earn a doctorate, write a book, and became a White House political appointee serving two presidents.

My education progressed through nursing school, Flight Nurse school, New Jersey City University, Yale, Columbia, and the Brookings Institution. I am very proud of my accomplishments; however, to be valuable they must be used to benefit society, such as students, veterans, elderly and others in the community, state and country.

As I mentioned reaching your goals and objectives in life and overcoming hurdles and challenges takes focus. And focus takes commitment and energy. We all know that we are surrounded in life by others and often they, also, require our attention and focus. You should reserve both of those for those most deserving. There are countless good people in the world. Many of them surround me. Truly good people—the kind you want to associate with—know there are other good people out there. It's the people that do not believe good exists you have to be wary of and you absolutely have to be cautious with those you think might be good but seem to always need something... are always looking for someone to help them or to care for or about them. You will want to comfort these people. Be a friend or lover to them... to be strong for them. But don't rush to do that out of reflex because you are so kind and good.

NEVER blindly believe a person is good.

Watch them.

Listen to them.

See how they act when it seems no one is watching them.

See how they treat others and most importantly, see how they feel about themselves (by their actions and words).

They have to prove to you that they are good.

If what you see is negative... if their view of themselves is destructive, self-defeating or they are always running down other people and lamenting their life. Or conversely they are over the top, overly enthusiastic about things (anything) when they surely don't have a basis to be that enthused. And never realize their thinking is distorted or comprehend they have a skewed perception of reality. Be cautious. Keep them at arm's length until they merit you letting them into your heart and your life. And if they don't improve, become considerate (of themselves and others), self-aware and rational. They continue the way they are. Keep them at a distance and let them deal with their own life. You can be friendly with them but don't owe them any part of your life. They have to earn the right to your highest level of friendship or love. Making the terrible mistake to take them in, trying to help them, accept or tolerate them and keep a relationship with them, opens you up to their bitterness and bile. And they will eat away at your time and if it continues and you let it... their negativity or irrationality will affect your life. They can drag you down. Don't let it happen. Only accept friends and relationships on your terms. Here is something that author Dennis Lowery wrote for his four, young, daughters but it holds true for men and women of all ages:

> *Confidence does not come from being in a group. And self-confidence does not come from becoming comfortable around others... Confidence comes from being comfortable with yourself.*

The best way you can help people is by having confidence in who you are and in what you plan for your life. That does not mean being selfish or self-centered; be an independent thinker and above the very neediness, negativity and irrationality I just pointed out for you. That makes you strong enough to protect yourself and makes you the truly good person that makes our world a better place to live.

Believing in Yourself Is Critical to Success

As a child, I followed the way my parents raised me and my brothers and sisters.

- They did it with love.

46

- They did it with respect.
- They did it with a willingness to undertake hard work because it was needed to be done for the family.

I learned when you come from not having anything when you finally have something it is truly a blessing. Coming up that way has created in me an appreciation of things and people; an appreciation that I hope I never lose or take for granted. I like and admire the finer things in life, but I've never chased them or felt that I needed them to be happy.

You have to have a centerpiece to build your life around, or perhaps better said... a compass that keeps you pointed in the right direction. Life buffets you. At times, it can be a harsh wind blowing from all corners. Without something within to give you the strength to bear the winds and to keep your equilibrium, you never know what direction you should go in, and can fall, never to get up.

I'm a deeply spiritual person but one that does not need to evangelize. I prefer quiet strength to loud superficiality; where talking is just for talking's sake. Our world seems to gravitate toward sound bites and short attention spans are mesmerized by flash and show. I believe that a life of value comes from a willingness to slow things down. To be someone of substance (and no I do not mean substance by way of material things), by taking the time to consider things before making decisions, speaking out or responding. To take the time to understand, ourselves is far more important than time spent puzzling over the meaning of everyone else.

"A tiny thing is Mankind, on the scale of the Universe, but in some people their soul is the Universe."

— Dennis Lowery

We are all small in the grand scheme of things, but some have within us the power to make our reality much larger… much more complete and to our liking. We see not just who we are, but who we can become. We appreciate what we have yet still reach toward a goal or objective. Stretching ourselves. Those of us who were not born perfect know that each day of our life is an opportunity to learn more, do more and be more. Even if it's only a small step. A bit of progress or when your personal circle of enlightenment expands slightly to push back the shadows and darkness of the path ahead and that borders the sides of the road we travel in life.

We are individuals. We are also part of a much greater whole. But our dreams and ambitions, though we may share them, are uniquely ours. We own them. And sometimes, good or bad, they own us. So it is, collectively, with humans. We're all in this together. But here's what you must hold dear and close: it's your life - your world - your universe. Make of it what you will and take heart as you do.

* * *

"The delicate balance of mentoring someone is not creating them in your own image, but giving them the opportunity to create themselves."
— Steven Spielberg

Sometimes a mentor is needed to show you something of the road ahead. They can be a spark of light or a steady beam that illuminates the way. Or at least sheds light on things you need to look closer at and give a thought to.

There's a point of light in every soul…
That can reveal a path to follow.
It may be a road that twists and turns.
And at times can feel like you've lost the way.

But the light reveals more as you go.
And you will find yourself with every step.
Seeing sights and scenes, you would never witness.
If you had not pushed beyond the dark.
Beyond the bend in the road.

— Dennis Lowery

Mentors have helped me throughout my life. They can help anyone and not just when we face those decision points where our life's road forks and we have to choose: go right, go left or go nowhere. They are also crucial during the many intermediate steps along the way.

You see, without a guiding hand or solid advice, sometimes we can falter, we may hesitate or even stop. We look ahead into the unknown and second-guess everything; our previous choices and even our abilities. I've faced many decisions and hard choices in my life. I know my mentors helped me to make the best decision I could at the time and often were the reason I kept putting one foot in front of the other. Sometimes they saw things in me, capabilities that I didn't see in myself.

This is what I believe and the advice I have for young people, whether you are beginning your career, advancing your career or looking for a career change:

First, you must take care of yourself and maintain a balance, that is physical, mentally, socially, economically, politically and spiritually (don't forget to pray) beneficial to you.

Second, in order to become successful, you must get a good education. Education was the hope of the past and it is surely the hope for the future. Education is a tool that empowers people to be better performers, communicators, supervisors, managers, and citizens. Education is the great liberator! Remember education is a journey, NOT a destination.

Third, do your very best in the job that you have. You may not be able to change the world, but you can shine a light where you are!

Fourth, you must visualize the future and dare to be a part of it! Say to yourself. "My contributions are important and I will be a part of this great nation's future."

Career Progression by Decade from 1970 to 2014

The 1970s

Maimonides Medical Center, Home Care Department

During this decade, my desire was to return to college for a degree in nursing. It took me ten years (1959 to 1969) to do so since I was helping to financially support my parents on the farm and my siblings in high school and college. During that time, I had positions of increased responsibility. I became a charge nurse, a nurse supervisor, a nurse manager and eventually rose to acting Home Health Agency Administrator.

While working as an administrator, I looked at the nursing degree requirements, curriculum and class schedules of various universities. I decided to attend New Jersey City University (NJCU) in the evenings to obtain a degree since this was the best option financially and for my schedule. At that time, nurses received sixty credits for a 3-year diploma, which was helpful toward the degree requirements. Two other nurses, Marjorie Greenridge and Muriel

Bushelle, from the medical center I worked at also attended NJCU with me. We enjoyed the university environment, the diversity of students, and the company of nursing colleagues. Though not quite the main attraction and appeal, we also loved music classes and that we could easily park in the student lots.

While at New Jersey City University, my colleagues and I frequently discussed attending graduate school and seeking nursing positions with more responsibility. As we discussed this option, an NJCU professor suggested that we check the bulletin board each day for possible scholarship opportunities.

I took that to heart and a few months before my graduation from NJCU, in May 1971, I noticed a flyer from Yale University on the bulletin board offering graduate scholarships for students in several professional areas.

I contacted the Yale University Admission Office for additional information related to their Masters in Public Health program (MPH). I visited Yale, talked to numerous faculty members and students, and then applied officially for admission. I had good fortune during my visit; the first person I met was Professor John Thompson, a nurse well-known for his research, innovation, and policy development.

I was accepted for admission and entered the MPH program in August 1971 with full tuition and a stipend for two years. I rented an apartment near the Divinity School on Whitney Avenue and took the Yale shuttle bus to classes. To help with finances, I also worked at a nursing home on weekends and flew as an Aero Medical Evacuation crew member on military aircraft as a Flight Nurse.

While at Yale, I enjoyed my graduate studies, the campus, colleagues and faculty members. I also enjoyed the physical fitness facilities especially playing squash. My experience at Yale was excellent, inspiring and challenging. But it was NJCU that inspired and helped me discover and obtain a bridge to graduate school.

On graduation in 1973 with a Master's in Public Health from Yale, I returned to Queens, New York. I was employed at Our Lady of Mercy Medical Center, Bronx, New York as Nurse Coordinator and Consultant for Psychiatry and Nursing.

For the next 5 years, I agonized about pursuing a doctorate degree, but the question was what type: EdD, PhD., ScD, DNP, DNS, DrPH or perhaps a law degree. While considering which doctorate to pursue, I was employed as coordinator and consultant to Nursing and Psychiatry departments, and instructor at New York Medical College working with nursing and medical students.

After reviewing research literature and several doctoral programs in NYC. I decided to pursue the Doctor of Education (EdD) at Teachers College, Columbia University. Based on the curriculum, tuition support and the convenience of class schedules and that I could make fit around my work schedule. I had a wonderful time studying at Columbia, collaborated with brilliant students and met numerous inspiring and influential faculty members.

I give high praise to the Department of Aging and the American Red Cross (ARC) in NYC for assisting with my doctoral dissertation. While researching for my dissertation, I collected data and information that both agencies could use to help improve services for the elderly. Since then, I have been a lifelong supporter of ARC by donating blood, funds and volunteering my time.

Educational Cake with
University Graduations, 1983

In the mid-1970s, after completing high school, my brother Jack, brother number five, came from Aiken to New York to work and spend the summer with me. He had decided to become a chicken farmer but changed his mind suddenly after his return to South Carolina at the end of the season. He returned home and called me one week later, stating he wanted to attend college, but needed $1200 immediately. Because of obligations to help others and investing in my own education, I had only saved $1400 over many years. I thought about what he had asked for and wondered if I should take this risk since he was not a good student in 12th grade. But after much thought and family consultation I made a decision. I believed strongly (and still do) that those who can help others... should; especially family members. I sent him the $1200.

He enrolled in college, transferred to Washington three years later, completed and received his degree then on went to finish medical school. He joined the Air Force, becoming a gastroenterologist and flight surgeon. This investment paid off and convinced me that when we invest in people, we reap benefits for a lifetime. Jack shared his success and helped numerous family members to reach their goals and become successful, too. There is a domino (some might say ripple) effect when we help people that are worthy of our aid.

Two years later, my brother number six, Lafayette expressed a desire to attend pilot training. To prepare him for school, we enrolled him in pilot training at the local airport in Aiken. Within six months, he completed ground school and received his private pilot license. Subsequently, he was admitted and graduated from the Embry-Riddle Aeronautical University flying program.

The 1980s

There were numerous opportunities to serve and participate in unique assignments with the Air Force and Air National Guard. In February 1980, I was offered an unexpected assignment by the New York Air National Guard (NYANG) as a charge nurse at the 1980 Olympic clinic. February through March 1980, I was a major assigned as Assistant Chief Nurse to the 105th TAC Hospital NYANG, White Plains, New York. I participated along with a select group of New York Militia personnel on active duty as a member of the Poly Olympic Medical Clinic in support of the 1980 Winter Olympics in Lake Placid, New York. We all flew up to Lake Placid on Ski C-130 airplane (this aircraft has wheels and skis for landing in arctic conditions). The event was a world-class international experience with numerous opportunities to network, to enhance my personal and professional development and use clinical skills in icy conditions. The weather was frigid, reaching temperatures seventy below zero with high winds at intervals. We had an opportunity to meet and observe many of the Olympic athletes in action.

During this decade, I continued to serve on numerous civilian and military committees. Also, I returned to college graduating with a doctorate and 2nd master's degree from Teachers College, Columbia University in 1983.

At this point in my career, in 1982, I had many questions about policies in nursing: education RN-BSN, quality of care, certification, business opportunities and the working environment. I consulted the ANA on my many concerns. ANA is the only full-service professional organization representing the interests of the nation's 3.4 million registered nurses through its constituent and state nurses' associations and its organizational affiliates. One day when discussing an issue with an ANA staff member, they asked me "Why don't you apply to work for ANA to help solve nursing issues?" I thought that since the ANA is the national professional organization for nurses they should already have people internally doing this, not me. I expressed my concerns at this point with a colleague, an Army nurse colonel. She said she had the same concerns and was considering going to work for ANA on educational issues.

In August 1985, ANA offered me a position as Senior Staff Specialist: Social and Economic Policy, Policy Development and Strategic Planning Division in Kansas City, Missouri. My job was to work to resolve some of the issues that I had concerns over the years in coordination with other staff members. After being at the ANA just over two years, I was presented with another leadership opportunity.

At that time, I was the Chief Nurse Executive for the 105th TAC Medical Clinic and struggling to recruit nurses. The unit was going from small 0-2 search airplanes and C130 cargo types to C5A jumbo jets (similar to a 747 commercial jet). These planes carried a cargo of tanks, buses, and trucks. The 2nd level upstairs was the passenger compartment. These aircraft required increased medical personnel, extensive training, and more flying crew. I was asked by my commanding officer, the group commander (GC) Major General Paul Weaver, Jr., to make two recommendations for qualified personnel to take command of the medical clinic. This commander assignment was historically held by male physicians with flight surgeon wings. Which I did—submitting to him the two best-qualified officers based on my experience and in my judgment. The result of my recommendations was unexpected. General Weaver told me. "Here I am, with you following orders, doing your job by recommending suitable officers to take command of the clinic. When it hit me. The best candidate was right in front of me."

When General Weaver offered me the command, I was totally in shock. A command of this type historically went to white male physicians. No females had ever commanded a clinic or hospital unit—for him to offer it to me, an African-American woman, no matter how well qualified—was a startling thing. But there were some considerations about my accepting the command. The unit inspection report was not very good. It meant spending more time in New York (I was living in and commuting from Kansas City at the time). There was a shortage of medical and nursing staff and I was happy at ANA.

But this was an opportunity I could not pass up. I had to accept it. Nationally, there were some unhappy medical personnel due to this decision, but ultimately it benefited many other professionals such as nurses, dentists, biomedical and other medical service corps officers. This decision opened the door to those whom would not have had an opportunity to serve as a commander. The GC had the support of the senior officials of the National Guard at the Pentagon. And in 1986, I was appointed the commander of the 105th USAF Medical Clinic in Newburgh, New York.

I was determined to be successful in the position and was. And that earned me yet another stepping-stone to new opportunities. In spite of some medical organizations being unhappy with my assignment, we were able to recruit medical and flying personnel, improve the readiness status and meet global mission requirements. By all measures, we had improved performance under my command. I was requested to present my experience at the Aerospace Medical Association Convention (which included flight surgeons and flight nurses), to active duty Air Force, National Guard, and Reserve Chief Nurse Executives. I discussed my experience with lessons learned, successful models and best practices. I also discussed those initiatives that did not work. I stressed that this assignment, my command, was successful because of the team effort and a key senior executive that embraced change and opportunities for all professionals to excel as leaders. This was a challenging time. Just think all this took place while was helping ANA resolve some policy issues and the opportunity, in part, I believe was aided by my participation with ANA.

Soon after this experience, I noted a vacancy announcement for an active duty position at Headquarters United States Air Force, Office of the Surgeon General, for an Air National Guard nurse. The position included but was not limited to a review of nursing policies, education, and access to health care and to enhance collaboration between active duty, guard, and reserve components. The nurse in this office was leaving to attend a senior service school for a year. It was a coveted assignment.

After much discussion with ANA leaders and senior nurses in Washington, I competed for the position. I was selected and subsequently relocated to Washington DC as ANG Assistant to the

Director for Medical Readiness and Nursing Services. From July 1987 to February 1993 as an active duty, Colonel, United States Air Force, Office of the Surgeon General, Bolling Air Force Base.

My assignment was to coordinate headquarters-level health policy, program development, congressional hearings, and information systems issues with senior representatives of DoD, regulatory agencies, federal and civilian executive organizations. Organize and chair workgroups on leadership, readiness, and education. Design and conduct a worldwide survey on unmet health needs of women in the Air Force including access to services and benefits. This study based on follow-up showed a twenty percent increase in access to health care.

During my time in this assignment, I advised the Surgeon General on ANG policy and served as Military Representative on the Secretary of Defense's Committee, Defense Advisory Committee on Women in the Services (DACOWITS).

The 1990s

Bolling Air Force Base, 1991

I was very happy as I rose through the ranks in the Air National Guard and Air Force. As a woman and a minority, I was pleased and even content when I made "bird" colonel. I had even considered putting in my retirement papers thinking I was at the end of where my wings could take me.

I was shocked, one day, when I got a call from the National Guard personnel department at the Pentagon. They told me that my name was on the selection list to be considered to become a General Officer. I didn't even know what that meant and had had to ask them. I was on active duty at the time at Bolling Air Force Base sitting in my little cubicle. I had made full colonel a few years before and been a Flight Nurse, a Flight Nurse Examiner, a hospital commander and now was in the Surgeon General's office. All positions I had reached through hard work and I was very proud of what I'd done. But my current assignment was up in less than a year and I had decided I would retire while on active duty and not return to Guard status.

That phone call changed everything. Pentagon personnel told me what was involved just to be included on the selection list. I would have to go to a meeting at the Pentagon and be interviewed. I would be investigated and cleared for top security clearance and they would talk with significance individuals in my past. I had to provide my life's history in detail. All that became a package of paperwork just to be on the list for consideration to be selected for promotion to one-star General Officer rank. And I was only one person from several throughout the National Guard. I thought, no way I'll make it. But I also believed since I was on the list I should do everything I could to try and make it happen. If it didn't, I was still happy having made it to bird (full) colonel and to have worked at a senior high level on important issues for the Air National Guard and Air Force. If I did not make it I would go ahead and retire and be happy with my accomplishments.

Then a few months later I received another call from the Pentagon. The selection board had just met and they wanted to see me. I thought this was a routine thing; part of the check off list for everyone being considered. But anyway I asked why they needed to see me. They told me because you were selected. I couldn't believe it! That told me that now bigger range me were swarming for my new position. I was speechless. One General Officer position open—officers across the country on the list competing for it and I was selected. I had to ask them why I was chosen. "You have flight experience. You've shown increasing levels of responsibility. You got your master's and doctorate degrees. You've taught at a senior level, and you've commanded a hospital and worked in the Surgeon General's office. We also looked at your civilian career and all that you've accomplished. You've earned it." I was still in shock as they continued. "You'll be the first African-American female General Officer in the history of the National Guard."

It struck me hard then. How in the world could a black girl from a cotton field in South Carolina become a General in the Air National Guard/Air Force? I shook my head at the thought.

I talked to my brother who had also become an Air Force officer. I told him, "They picked me... I'm going to be a general." He was quiet for a moment and then said, "You sure that's what you heard them say?" It was still hard for me to believe, too. I didn't tell anyone else; I wanted to see it in writing with signed orders. Once I did, I made what seemed 1000 copies to share with friends and family.

My promotion and pinning ceremony was at the Pentagon in the conference room. One of my mentors and also a General Officer, Paul Weaver, pinned on one of my stars. It was an incredible experience.

Promotion to Major General,
Bolling AFB, Washington, DC,
Pinning by Lt Gen Russell Davis
& Maj Gen Paul Weaver,
Sept. 1, 1998

As a new general, you attend General Officer Orientation making the circuit of several military bases and commands, like SAC, MAC, TAC (former command designations). And also go through training and indoctrination in ethics and politics which also become important aspects of the new rank. It was an indescribably great feeling and experience.

At the General Officer Orientation, there were only two females out of the thirty-six new one-star Generals. During my orientation, I knew that I had to be sharp. So I talked to my senior enlisted, my sergeants. They knew the ropes for everything I needed to know. I had learned early in my military career to treat people fairly and you can rely on them to help you. I called on them for what I needed to know as I became a general. I listened to them and that made the transition easier.

Later on I found some of my now lower-ranking colleagues were hesitant to speak to me. I asked them why. They replied, "We don't like to talk to Generals!"

Shortly afterward, I left active duty Air Force and returned to reserve status and the civilian world. I had considered working for a defense contractor or IBM. But I decided to join the Department of Veterans Affairs (VA). I heard about many issues related to the quality of care, women veterans' access to VA benefits and services and not being treated with dignity and respect. I wanted to address women veterans concerns and other issues in the veterans' systems that needed attention. I wanted to help fix veterans' policy and services issues.

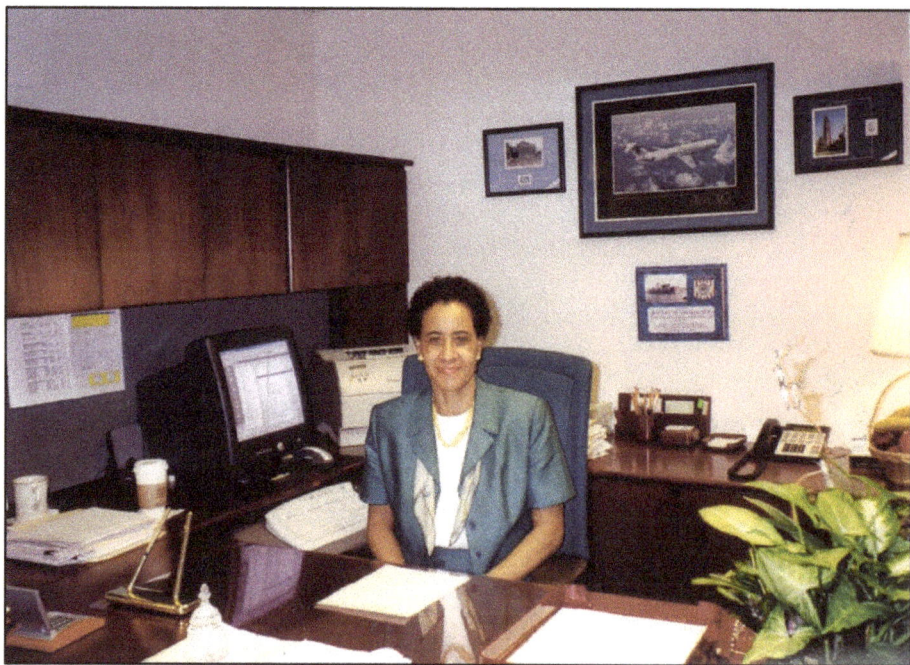

VA Office, 2002

I was employed as Director, Patient Care Inspections and Program Evaluation, Office of Healthcare Inspections, Department of Veterans Affairs, Office of Inspector General from August 1993 to July 2001. During my assignment, among other duties and responsibilities, I managed a Congressionally-mandated nation-wide program on Quality Assurance/Quality Improvement, clinical inspections. And conducted oversight of VA hospitals, ambulatory care and community-based clinics, nursing homes and domiciliaries (about 1400 facilities at that time). I directed a multidisciplinary staff of inspectors responsible for conducting oversight reviews to improve the economy, effectiveness, and efficiency of VA programs nationally.

In my position working for the Inspector General, I looked at the quality of care and management issues nationally. Every three years each of the over 150 VA facilities had to be visited and evaluated. I enjoyed the challenges of the job. I especially tried to focus on women's issues since there were many that needed to be addressed.

My IG experience was helpful because it gave me skills to immediately identify an issue, generate solutions and follow through to be sure the solutions were implemented.

I had been with the VA Office of Inspector General for eight years when I got another, equally surprising, phone call. I was told I'd been put on a list of possible political appointees to be the Director of the Center for Women Veterans. It had been established by Congress in November 1994 by Public Law (P.L.) 103-446. Its mission was to:

- Monitor and coordinate VA's administration of health care and benefits services, and programs for women Veterans.
- Serve as an advocate for a cultural transformation (both within VA and in the general public) in recognizing the service and contributions of women Veterans and women in the military.

- Raise awareness of the responsibility to treat women Veterans with dignity and respect.

As its director, I would become a member of the Senior Executive Service (SES) and White House political appointee. I told them that I had not applied for that position. They replied that it was not one you can apply for; someone had to nominate me. And if I were selected I could choose not to accept it. I asked them who had nominated me. They wouldn't tell me and I never found out. All they would say was that it came from within the Secretary of Veterans Affairs office. They said I needed to speak with the White House VA liaison. Which I did and found out that the position meant I would be advising the Secretary of Veterans Affairs on women veterans' issues and representing the VA at the White House on the Council on Women and Girls. A very senior job with a lot of responsibilities. I was competing with others who had been nominated. And as a political appointment it started a new, even more, intensive round of scrutiny into my qualifications and background.

Again I thought, no way. I had not been aware the position even existed and I was only remotely politically connected at that level. Yet two months later I received a phone call that I had been selected. Again, I was dumbfounded I'd been picked. And again, a flashback to standing in the cotton field —it seemed not so long ago. Yes, I was a general and had achieved high rank but this was something else—a different level entirely. This was a White House appointee position and meant working a great deal with politicians and their staffs. I would have to go to Capitol Hill and testify before Congress. I would have to meet and work with congressional members, brief the Secretary of Veterans Affairs and White House officials on women veterans' issues. I would be addressing all kinds of questions on domestic public policy and VA processes in a way I had never had to deal with before. It'll be all this they told me and then asked, "Do you want to accept the position?" I asked back, "How long can I think about it?" "You don't have any time; we need to know now," I said, "Okay, I will try it for two years." They replied, "No—it's for six years. The only way to get out sooner is to resign for good reason or do something wrong and you get fired."

As director, I served as the primary advisor to Secretary of Veterans Affairs on all matters related to programs, issues, legislation, and initiatives for and affecting women veterans. As Director of the Center for Women Veterans (CWV), I worked to ensure that female veterans are aware of their benefits and services available to them. Including health care, education, counseling, insurance, and home and business loans. Services to female veterans will become increasingly important as the proportion of women in the military increases.

> Women in 2001 constituted 7.5 percent (1.8 million) of the nation's 23.4 million living veterans. And the percentage will increase for two reasons. First, because the number of women in active service has risen, to 17 percent; and second, because male veterans, mostly from World War II, are dying at a rate of 1,400 per day. As of October 7, 2014, there are 2.29 million women veterans, about 10 percent, of the 22 million total veteran population in this country. See reference: Department of Veterans Affairs, Table 6L: VetPop 2011, at http://www.va.gov/vetdata/

When I accepted the position as director CWV, my immediate supervisor didn't want me to leave on short notice. It meant short-term that his job would become harder. But his supervisor was happy because he believed good people should have opportunities to move up and take on greater roles in making changes. I told my supervisor that my staff was well trained and that I knew several experienced nurse executives that I could recommend taking my position. That made him feel better as we planned a two-week transition. Then he received a call from the White House VA liaison that they wanted me to start the next week.

I scrambled and worked through the week and weekend to finish cases and to get moved into my new office by the following Monday. That Wednesday I got a call from the Secretary of the VA's Chief of Staff that I was to accompany her to a luncheon and then a veterans' group meeting. That morning I traveled to the luncheon with the Chief of Staff to have her tell me, "I'm dropping you off after the lunch and not going to the meeting." I was being thrown right into the fire or maybe with a group of very unhappy veterans. After the lunch Chief of Staff waved, said "bye," and sped off. I was on my own.

I went to the veterans group meeting to be faced with some very unhappy women of all ranks and services. They were dissatisfied at the lack of response and action from the Secretary's office and that they were being treated with a lack of dignity and respect. They had a whole list of issues and also handed me a copy of their last meeting minutes which covered discussion on those same concerns.

I read them and then heard them out until they finished covering all of their grievances. I explained I was only on my third day in this new position but that some of their problems they had brought up previously and I was aware of from working with the Inspector General's office. I told them I would go back to the VA and work on each issue they brought up and would come back to their next meeting with answers and action on those I could address and the status on those that were still being worked. I would tell them what things that could not be done immediately because of VA policy or legislative reasons. On those which we needed to change procedures to fix the problem, with the Advisory Committee on Women Veterans and their help, we would submit proposals for new legislation or policy changes. If that were what was needed, I would consult with VA officials to work on policy proposals and new laws.

The veterans group immediately put me on the spot and asked, "Why do you think you can handle some of these health issues. What makes you feel you can help?" I told them about my various experiences. "I've been a nurse for decades. I have my doctorate. I'm a veteran and as a General Officer worked with the Inspector General's office for over eight years. It's not been easy, as you can imagine, accomplishing the things that I have and I have solved problems along the way. I'll take all of that experience and apply to your issues. Some I know we can fix. Others will take more help; some we may need policy changes. Between now and the next meeting I will send you a progress report on what I've done—what is still in work—and what cannot be done without policy or legislation changes. Then we'll discuss all issues and concerns again at your next meeting." That action seemed to calm committee members and our meeting ended on a positive note.

I returned to my office and got to work. A few weeks later I sent the veterans group a detailed issue by issue update on progress on where things stood. I followed up and called to ask the chair of the group when the next meeting was; as promised I wanted to update them in person. The organization's leader told me they were pleased with the progress and with my status report —I did not need to attend the meeting instead it was best if I just updated them periodically.

Others at the VA, including the Secretary's Chief of Staff, were amazed at the action and progress since the group had repeatedly contacted VA on various complaints and concerns. I replied, "Well, all I did was listen to them, take notes on every issue and then came back here. I worked on them and sent them a detailed progress report to let them know what was going on with updates. They were satisfied with that and as long as I keep working on the issues and updating them I believe they will continue to be satisfied."

And that's what I and my office staff did as a collaborative team. I never had another call or complaint from that veterans group. And this is a good example of something I believe in. When in front of someone or a group, you face them, and tell them honestly what you can and can't do for them—and then deliver. It's not just the usual all talk and no action... and they appreciate that.

The Secretary's Advisory Committee on Women Veterans met three times a year and I invited veterans' service organizations to attend the meetings. I wanted them included and wanted their input and participation. That was important because part of my duties was attending the White House Council on Women and Girls and Secretary of VA Senior Staff meetings and providing that information verbally and in written reports. It was an important part of making all parties aware of what the issues were and what was being done to address them. Many of these reports were also posted on the White House and the VA websites for people to read and become aware of what we were doing regarding issues about women veterans.

The White House Council on Women and Girls consisted of twenty-nine federal agencies and other organizations jointly working together addressing women's issues including women veterans' issues. That was the common thread throughout that we needed to be sure we were aware of and address issues without duplicating efforts. This cross-agency and cross-department cooperation were something I enjoyed as we were working together for the common good of veterans from all services.

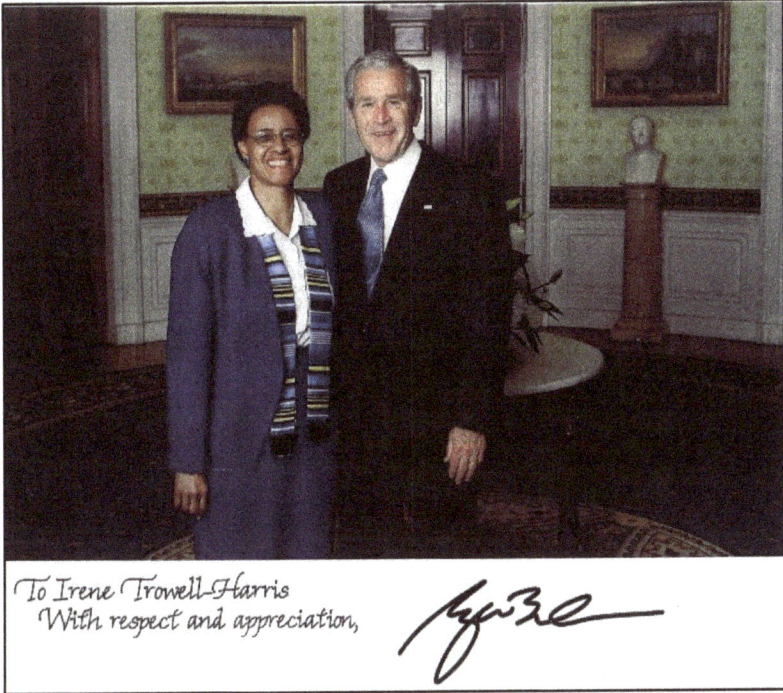

To Irene Trowell-Harris
With respect and appreciation,

Veterans Day Photo with President George W. Bush, 2006

I also enjoyed the social outreach aspect of working with the White House. I would attend some events hosted by First Lady Laura Bush such as local schools book fairs and festivals where she'd read to kids. I just love her; she did so many things to help children. When President Bush's presidential library opened in May 2013, I received a special invitation to attend and it was a wonderful experience to see First Lady Laura Bush again.

I remember attending meetings at the White House on Veterans Day and Memorial Day. There would be a special breakfast event for veterans at the White House and in the receiving line each veteran would get a few personal moments with the president and on occasions with the First Lady to take pictures. On Veterans Day, we could bring other veterans to the White House. They were from all services, eras of service and also different backgrounds. They would get to meet the president and this was a very special occasion for them and me. Afterward, we would be part of the president's and VA Secretary's team that visited Arlington Cemetery to honor our fallen. It was a somber and humbling experience for me and the veterans.

The time I spent at the White House and VA as a political appointee was a tremendous and rewarding experience. Six years went by very quickly and I was coming up to the end and expected to move on to another position or possibly even to consider retirement from government service. Then I received a call asking me to stay for another six years! I thought about all that had been done and all that still needed to be and decided to stay.

I remained through President Bush's second term and with the administration change expected I would leave as most political appointees do at that time. But I got a call from the VA White House Liaison for the incoming Obama administration, asking me to come talk to them about staying on in the position. We met and discussed that there were still many women's issues to work on and a great deal to be done. They asked me to hold off presenting the usual change of administration resignation letter for my position. At that point, they did not have a person to nominate and the job was too important to leave vacant.

THE WHITE HOUSE

WASHINGTON

January 20, 2009

Dr. Irene Trowell-Harris
Unit G
2582 South Arlington Mill Drive
Arlington, Virginia 22206

Dear Irene:

Laura and I thank you for serving in my Administration. We appreciate the long hours you put in to do your job, and we are grateful to you and your family for the many sacrifices you made on behalf of the American people.

We have made history together. We have worked to solve problems, instead of passing them on to future generations. We have made our country safer, stronger, and more secure. We have shown the world the compassion and generosity of our people. And we have supported freedom's march around the globe.

May God bless you.

Sincerely,

George W. Bush

Letter of Appreciation from President Bush 2009

Each president is different in their agenda and approach. With the change in administration from Bush to Obama, I wanted to be sure what I was doing, what I felt needed to be done for veterans, especially women, matched with the presidents' agenda. Both presidents and their staffs wanted veterans to be cared for as they should, based on their respective plans. The one difference in the Obama administration was they wanted more focus and effort from the White House to recognize the accomplishments of women veterans.

Veterans Day photo with President Barack Obama, 2012

In the past, there had been plenty of male veterans recognized by the White House but rarely, and few, women. Obama wanted to change that and women veterans wholeheartedly agreed. I helped implement programs to find women veterans deserving of recognition whether it was in combat, for their job performance or community work. We gathered names and nominations of veterans for all services across the country and the White House would then select fifteen to twenty to review and select those for recognition at the White House. This ceremony recognized them specifically for their accomplishments and service to the nation.

Another group never lauded or even acknowledged by any White House administration was the Tuskegee Airmen. A special ceremony was arranged to recognize their contribution to not only World War II combat, but also in breaking down racial stereotyping and barriers. I did not believe they had been intentionally omitted from presidential recognition—and this is probably true, to a degree, for women veterans, too—but was rather a case of, we never thought to do it. I think as a society; when it comes to race and gender equality, that we've moved from a stage of active denial that inequality exists to one of accepting that it does but overlooking it, to today where we're we've acknowledged it needs to be eliminated. We are seeing a transition to equal recognition being an 'always on' part of social consciousness, where there is not any excuse for intolerance. There are things from the past we need to redress and present and future things to move forward on, but we are making progress.

In 1998, I received a call from NGB Human Resources at the Pentagon informing me that my name came up on the two-star General Officer list. I was subsequently selected by the Review Board, promoted to Major General and assigned as Assistant to the Director, ANG for Human Resources Readiness representing 107,000 Guard members, at that time. I handled the readiness, mentoring, education, women and diversity issues, and support for part of the budget. I served on numerous committees including the ANG Board of Directors (Committee of Advisors) and chaired the National Human Resources Quality Board.

I served thirteen years in my position as Director of the Center for Women Veterans. That was unprecedented for a political appointee. I served under President Bush for eight years and then President Obama for his first term and well into the second before deciding to retire.

Also, in 1998, I became the first woman to have a Tuskegee Airmen, Inc. chapter named in my honor—the 'Major General Irene Trowell-Harris Chapter' in Newburgh, New York. In 1999, a mentoring award was named in my honor at the 105th Airlift Wing, Newburgh, New York.

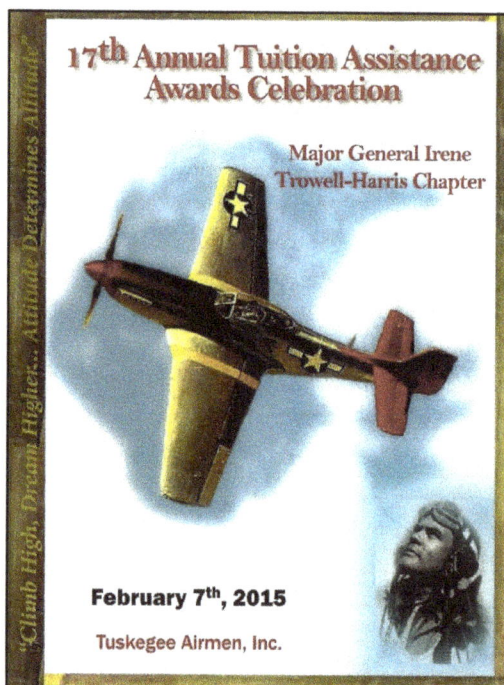

TAI Journal cover February 2015

The 2000s

In my new position, I incorporated women veterans' issues as part of a National Women's Agenda. I coordinated activities as the Designated Federal Officer for the Secretary of Veterans Affair's Advisory Committee on Women Veterans (ACWV). I presented testimony on Capitol Hill at intervals and submitted ACWV reports to Congress on women veterans' health care and benefits issues every two years.

During this time, I also represented the VA on the White House Council on Women and Girls and the Defense Advisory Committee on Women in the Services (DACOWITS). DACOWITS was established in 1951 by then Secretary of Defense, George C. Marshall. The Committee is composed of civilian women and men appointed by the Secretary of Defense. Members provide advice and recommendations on matters and policies relating to the recruitment and retention, treatment, employment, integration, and well-being of highly qualified professional women in the Armed Forces.

Beginning in 2002, the Committee began providing advice and recommendations on family issues related to recruitment and retention of a highly qualified professional military. Historically, DACOWITS' recommendations have been very instrumental in effecting changes to laws and policies addressing mutual interest items for women service members and veterans.

From 2010 to 2014

During this period, I was still serving as Director, Center for Women Veterans, on numerous policy, legislative, benefits and health care committees. But I was also considering retirement. My journey in life to that point had been about fulfilling a dream with advanced education and career progression. I had done that and achieved far more professionally than I ever imagined. When asked, by others, to describe my path I responded that my career flight made unscheduled stops, ran into turbulence, reached unexpected heights, and traveled internationally.

Even with barriers, I was able to reach senior levels in the private/civilian, military and federal service sectors. As a nurse: I progressed from staff nurse to a nurse manager, supervisor, and consultant and as Senior Staff Specialist, Social and Economic

Policy for the American Nurses Association. In the military I went from a 1st Lieutenant to Major General in positions such as Flight Nurse to instructor, to Flight Nurse Examiner (earning senior Flight Nurse wings with a star and wreath), to chief nurse executive, commander and advisor to chief nurse, Office of the Air Force Surgeon General. In federal service: I rose from GS 15 to Senior Executive Service for the Department of Veterans Affairs as a White House political appointee for two presidents.

During my tenure as White House (WH) political appointee, I was able to invite family members, co-workers, and VA staff members to the White House. We attended various events such as Easter Egg Roll for children, garden tours, and wounded warriors' programs, Memorial Day, Veterans Day reception, holiday tours, concerts and other activities. These were once in a lifetime educational experiences for many people.

* * *

Due to my lifelong interest and work with nursing policy issues, I established the Irene Trowell-Harris Endowed Leadership Fund at the American Nurses Foundation. Its purpose is to educate nurses using a systematic method to help improve the quality of care. And to support initiatives that give nurses a greater voice in influencing health care delivery and policy.

The American Nurses Foundation (ANF) is the charitable and philanthropic arm of the American Nurses Association (ANA). The Foundation supports programs that transform the nation's health through the power of nursing.

From the ANF News Release:

"Maj. Gen. Trowell-Harris's life is a lesson in leadership and generosity. She has used her passion for education, nursing,

and helping others throughout her remarkable career to advance the nation's health and well-being. Her own successes in nursing have enabled her to be a national role, model

Her investment in the work of the Foundation and ANA will enable us to ensure that nurses' expertise and insight have the greatest impact on health care," said ANF Executive Director Kate Judge.

"Investing in nurse leadership as a legacy is important to me for inspiring and educating future generations of nurse leaders to excel in the civilian, military and federal sectors," said Trowell-Harris. *"As a nurse, I was employed in the civilian, federal and military arenas which meant taking risks and learning the politics of each area. However, I had a passion for challenging assignments and was anxious to take risks to excel and help improve the system with policy changes. This was difficult at the time, but with extensive cooperation and collaboration with others the process did work. The goal was to improve the system while enhancing my professional competency skills. This goal was to concentrate on issues and solving problems not on serving the needs of any political party or political interests."*

THE WHITE HOUSE

WASHINGTON

February 9, 2015

Dr. Irene Trowell-Harris
Arlington, Virginia

Dear Irene:

Please know I deeply appreciate your dedication to my Administration. I trust you take pride in everything you have accomplished, and in all you have brought to the Department of Veterans Affairs.

By choosing public service, you carried on a noble, important tradition at the heart of some of America's greatest and most lasting achievements. The passion, skill, and professionalism of public servants help move our Nation forward and ensure we meet the high expectations of the citizens we serve.

Thank you for your service and for all you have done for my Administration and this country we love so much. As you take on new adventures, I wish you all the best.

Sincerely,

Letter of Appreciation from President Obama 2015

CHAPTER FOUR

CHALLENGING POLITICS AND NETWORKING FOR SUCCESS

"You have to learn the rules of the game. And then you have to play better than anyone else."

— Albert Einstein

My last few years in federal service were particularly meaningful to me because of the impact that can be made by people in senior positions in our government. And especially within departments and agencies such as the VA and other veterans and women-related organizations within the United States government working collaboratively on issues

The keys to working in politics successfully are in collaboration and coordination with other people and agencies with common interests and goals. Another key component is connecting people for cooperation through extensive networking. With my vast experiences working in the civilian sector, military, federal and political arenas, I had the opportunity to know and work with many people in various fields of expertise. My goal was to concentrate on issues and solving problems across party lines rather than serving the needs of any political party or political interests.

Over the course of my life, there have been numerous positive changes for all women including women veterans. The Department of Veterans Affairs, Center for Women Veterans, ACWV and Task Force on Women Veterans all contributed the to the progress of healthcare, benefits and services for women veterans.

The VA Advisory Committee on Women Veterans (ACWV) was established and chartered in November 1983 by Public Law 98-160. The Advisory Committee on Women Veterans assesses the needs of women Veterans, with respect to VA programs such as compensation, rehabilitation, outreach, health care, etc. The Committee reviews VA's programs, activities, research projects, and other initiatives designed to meet the needs of women Veterans. It makes recommendations to the Secretary on ways to improve, modify, and affect change in programs and services for women veterans and follows up on all those proposals.

The Veterans Task Force is a joint effort which led to the establishment of the Department-wide Women Veterans Program. Which an integrated, collaborative, transparent, cross-VA program to improve and enhance services and benefits delivery to women veterans. There are also examples of collaboration in government to honor women veterans.

The Department of Veterans Affairs and the White House acknowledged women veterans who made a difference. Fourteen women veterans from across the country were selected by the White House as a Women Veterans Champions of Change. Their contributions and sacrifices while serving in the military were often surpassed by the extraordinary things they are doing today to make a difference in their communities. They were honored in ceremonies hosted by the White House and the Department of Veterans Affairs on March 19, 2013:

"These women Veterans continued serving long after their military service," said First Lady Michelle Obama. *"It is about being part of something bigger*

than ourselves. It is the thread that connects everyone here. You served proudly. Now it is our turn to answer the call."

On March 11, 2009, President Obama signed an Executive Order creating the White House Council on Women and Girls. The mission of the Council is to provide a coordinated federal response to the challenges confronted by women and girls and to ensure that all Cabinet and Cabinet-level agencies consider how their policies and programs affect women and families.

New World of Experiences with International Speaking Opportunities

Traveling nationally and internationally is both an impressive education and enlightening experience. Global travel offers new avenues for learning about other people of the world and cultures. The United States Air Force, New York Air National Guard and Department of Veterans Affairs offered me the opportunity to travel to numerous states and countries overseas.

During my professional career, I was given an opportunity to serve on several international projects. In 1997, I served as the Air Force speaker representing the United States at the International Conference on Women in Defense in Johannesburg, South Africa. There I discussed my experience in military, leadership, DACOWITS and met with South Africa's Surgeon General and visited their nursing school with a senior female Army officer. Also, I was one of the 1997 Air Force representatives for the Committee on Women in the NATO Conference, Istanbul, Turkey. At the conference, we discussed mutual interest items with thirty-eight other countries such as education, leadership, mentoring, and collaboration models.

Dr. Irene Trowell-Harris

In 2008, I received an unexpected international assignment at VA. I represented the Secretary of Veterans Affairs and spoke at the November 2008 Fédération Mondiale des Anciens Combattants, World Veterans Fédération, Standing Committee on Women Meeting in Paris, France. I presented an overview of VA, health and benefits services, and the women veterans' program including key legislation. There were over 38 countries represented at this event.

PART 2

FAMILY & TRAVEL

"There is no such thing as a "broken family." Family is family and is not determined by marriage certificates, divorce papers, and adoption documents. Families are made in the heart. The only time family becomes null is when those ties in the heart are cut. If you cut those ties, those people are not your family. If you make those ties, those people are your family. And if you hate those ties, those people will still be your family because whatever you hate will always be with you."

— C. JoyBell C.

CHAPTER FIVE

THE IMPORTANCE OF FAMILY

"The bond that links your true family is not one of blood, but of respect and joy in each other's life."

— Richard Bach

I was born just two generations away from slavery.

My grandfather, Jim Trowell, was enslaved until he was in his early 20s. After the Civil War, a white family took him under its wing, bequeathing him 50 acres in South Carolina that my parents gradually enlarged into a 200-acre farm. I was born in that farmhouse in 1939. There have been good times and bad times in my life and in my family's lives. However, in the bad times I am reminded of this line from a poem, which inspired new hope in many black Americans:

> *"History, despite its wrenching pain, cannot be unlived, but if faced with courage, need not be lived again."*

— Maya Angelou

There was a time when the color of your skin affected how others perceived you in society. And, still today, though we've made great strides there are still issues we much correct and prevent. However, there is one thing that all of us, any person of any color, race or creed, has control over. Our inner sense of self-worth.

Value is relative. Many understand this, but there are those that don't grasp the concept. But there comes a time when intrinsic value is far greater than what people see; when what's inside is so much more important than what people see or think they see. It's who and what you are inside that establishes your worth—not the car you drive—not the opulence of your home or the money you have. I'll share with you a little story from Reverend Albert E. Sims that eloquently puts this message across:

A costly Diamond that had once sparkled in a lady's ring lay in a field amid tall grasses and oxeye daisies.

Just above it was a big Dewdrop that clung timidly to a nodding leaf.

Overhead, the blazing sun shone in all his noonday glory.

Ever since the first pink blush of dawn, the modest Dewdrop had gazed fixedly down upon the precious gem but feared to address a person of such exalted consequence.

At last, a large Beetle, during his rambles, chanced to espy the Diamond, and he also recognized him to be someone of high rank and importance.

"Sire," he said, making a low bow, "permit your humble servant to offer you greeting."

"Tha—nks," responded the Diamond in languid tones of affectation.

As the Beetle raised his head from his profound bow, his gaze happened to alight upon the Dewdrop.

"A relative of yours, I presume, Sire?" he remarked affably, waving one of his feelers in the direction of the Dewdrop.

The Diamond burst into a rude, contemptuous laugh.

"Quite too absurd, I declare!" he exclaimed loftily. "But there, what can you expect from a low, groveling beetle? Away, sir, pass on! Your very presence is distasteful to me. The idea of placing ME upon the same level—in the same family, as a low-born, mean, insignificant, utterly valueless—" Here the Diamond fairly choked for breath.

"But has he not beauty exactly like your own, Sire?" the Beetle ventured to interpose though with a very nervous air.

"BEAU—TY!" flashed the Diamond, with fine disdain—"the impudent fellow merely apes and imitates ME. However, it is some small consolation to remember that 'Imitation is the sincerest flattery.' But, even allowing him to possess it, mere beauty without rank is ridiculous and worthless. A Boat without water—a Carriage, but no horses—a Well, but never a winch: such is beauty without rank and wealth! There is no real worth apart from rank and wealth. Combine Beauty, Rank, and Wealth, and you have the whole world at your feet. Now you know the secret of the world worshipping ME."

And the Diamond sparkled and gleamed with vivid, violet flashes so that the Beetle was glad to shade his eyes.

The poor Dewdrop had listened silently to all that had passed and felt so wounded, that at last he wished he never had been born. Slowly a bright tear fell and splashed the dust.

Just then, a Skylark fluttered to the ground and eagerly darted his beak at the Diamond.

"Alas!" he piped, with a great sob of disappointment. "What I thought to be a precious dewdrop is only a worthless diamond. My throat is parched for want of water. I must die of thirst!"

"Really? The world will never get over your loss," sneered the Diamond.

But a sudden and noble resolve came to the Dewdrop. Deeply did he repent his foolish wish. He could now lay down his life that the life of another might be saved!

"May I help you, please?" he gently asked.

The Lark raised his drooping head.

"Oh, my precious, precious friend, if you will, you can save my life!"

"Open your mouth then."

And the Dewdrop slid from the blade of grass, tumbled into the parched beak, and was eagerly swallowed.

"Ah—well, well!" pondered the Beetle as he continued his homeward way. "I've been taught a lesson that I shall not easily forget. Yes, yes!

Simple worth is far better than rank or wealth without modesty and unselfishness—and there is no real beauty where these virtues are absent!"

— Rev. Albert E. Sims

Here is where what I just shared with you connects with family. It's how my personal values were formed in life.

I grew up with the family philosophy that we helped and cared about each other: religious colleagues, classmates, family members including brothers, sisters, aunts, uncles, grandparents and others. We were all worthy of mutual respect and love. We shared with others without expecting anything in return for helping them. It was understood that each person would help someone when the opportunity became available.

My parents came from humble beginnings. They did not have health insurance, indoor plumbing, a bank account, or any of the material things that signify what became known as the achieving the American Dream. But they had unconditional love and an insatiable desire to help their children become successful in life through a sound religious foundation and education.

Since my parents mainly worked on the farm, they both retired with small social security income. My siblings and I, usually starting in high school when we could get paying jobs, contributed to our parents throughout their life. Some of my brothers and sisters lived near them, visited frequently, helped on the farm, in their elder years assisted with their care and shopped for them when needed. Some gave money at intervals and one brother built them a new 3-bedroom house with assistance from siblings. After completing nursing school and living away from home and learning about life in general. I knew I had to help improve the family situation. I wanted to help them with health insurance, to open bank accounts, provide money to continue my siblings' education, to upgrade plumbing, and participate in recreation such as travel and social events. The first step was to send my parents a check monthly to help cover the usual household bills such as health and life insurance, clothing, heating fuel, car and farm equipment maintenance.

When I went to work at Talmadge Hospital in Augusta and received my first check in October 1959, I was ecstatic. From then on, I sent my parents a check monthly for almost 50 years. When I was traveling overseas, I would send them the checks pre-dated with a note to wait until the second of the month to cash or deposit the check. My father died in September 1998 and mother in January 2008. She died prior to signing her last check.

My parent's, despite their situation, tried to provide for and plan the family future when possible. There wasn't much they could do financially, but they gave us help and examples in others ways. Let me tell you an example of their preparing for the future. In her later years, my mother was well aware that she would be transitioning to another level of life at some point in the not too distant future. She planned well for her journey. Over 15 years before her death, in August 1993 she selected her coffin, including the color and model number. To make sure we got it right, she specified that she wanted to be buried in her white usher uniform with her Union Progress Society pin, and she even selected the color of her flowers. A few years before passing, she divided her property among the children because she did want any disagreements after her death. She told us that her bags were packed and she was well prepared for her journey because her work on Earth was done.

Upon her death at age 90, instead of flowers the family requested donations be made to the Aiken County Historical Museum for the education of students about history. The museum established the Irene Battle Trowell Memorial Education Fund in her honor. The purpose of this fund is to educate children at all grade levels in the county and contiguous areas of history. Children get an opportunity to go to the museum and experience history including military and veterans' history. The museum displayed a family exhibit for a few months of four generations of the Trowell family with photographs and a wall scroll of the families.

Family Photo Exhibit, Aiken County Historical Museum, Nov. 2007

Family Photo Exhibit, Aiken County Historical Museum, Nov. 2007

Family photo in front of Aiken County Historical Museum, Nov. 2007

As a family, we celebrate births, marriages, weddings, graduations, promotions, retirements, family reunions, even deaths. When my mother passed away, she requested that we celebrate her life's work of dedication to family, community, and church. She and my father raised their own eleven children and seventeen special needs children; those children that usually no one wanted to care for since many were ill or had disabilities. She also served in her church for over seventy years in various positions such as society secretary, teacher, usher, and a housemother. Family values, unity and support from the entire community clearly empowered her children to become successful. I learned that family must always be there to help parents, siblings, nieces and nephews.

In 1964, my younger sister came to live with me in NYC. She attended school and completed her nursing education and then had a very successful career. She retired after 35 years as a nurse and relocated to Florida with her family.

Through nurses, I worked with a New York Hospital and the Air National Guard I learned about how important it was to be educated about retirement planning, saving and investing in the stock market. This was very important. It enabled me to help siblings attend college, to send support to parents and nieces and nephews. And much later in life, to have recently established an Endowed Leadership Fund with the American Nurses Foundation, which will be discussed later in this book.

For a short while, my brother Jack came to live with me in New York. That summer he lived with me I took him on his first airplane ride with American Airlines during an open house at LaGuardia Airport in New York. But it was not long before he became tired of working low-income jobs and decided to attend college. Jack returned to Aiken, South Carolina, applied to several colleges and was admitted in August 1966 to the biology pre-medical program at Claflin University in Orangeburg, South Carolina.

> Founded in 1869 after the American Civil War by Northern missionaries for the education of freedmen and their children, Claflin is the oldest historically black college or university (HBCU) in the state of South Carolina. In 2014, it was ranked by Washington Monthly as the best liberal arts college in South Carolina, and by US News & World Report as the ninth-best HBCU in the nation.

When he received his acceptance notice, he called me because he did not have tuition for college. I only had $1,400 in my savings account and he needed $1,200 to start school. I withdrew the $1,200 from my savings account and sent Jack the money for college.

Jack entered college and did very well academically. He transferred in his junior year to Howard University in Washington, DC and graduated in May 1970. He was admitted to the Howard University Medical School in the fall of 1970 and graduated in May 1974 with a Doctor of Medicine (MD). Jack then joined the United States Air Force and completed subspecialty training on an Air Force Fellowship in Gastroenterology. He served on active duty as a Major and Chief, Division of Gastroenterology, Department of Medicine, Malcolm Grow USAF Medical Center, at Andrews Air Force Base, Maryland. He served in the Air Force Reserve and as a flight surgeon in the New York Air National Guard.

My brother Lafayette graduated from Aiken High School (an integrated school) in 1973 and was accepted at Embry-Riddle Aeronautical University in Daytona, Florida for pilot training. I traveled from New York to Aiken, South Carolina to accompany him since this was a new experience for him and his first major travel event. Flight training was very expensive and since Lafayette did not have a scholarship I paid several thousand dollars during the year for his tuition. At that time, I was working in New York as a head/nurse manager and on flying status with the New York Air National Guard. Even with two jobs and overtime at the hospital intervals, it was challenging, since Jack was in medical school and Lafayette in pilot training during the same period. Lafayette was an honor student and graduated with his wings. After graduation, he served as a flight instructor at Embry-Riddle and now owns a very successful satellite, electronic and TV business in Aiken.

Other siblings Lee, Crey, Franklin, and Sherry Diane pursued small business ventures such as in long-distance trucking, landscaping, construction and contracting, cement finishing, and satellite electronics or careers in professions such as law enforcement. They all still reside in Aiken. Frances lives in Queens, New York, pursued law enforcement as her career and is now retired from the NYC police department.

My sister, Mae had some difficulty deciding on her career path after completing high school in Aiken, South Carolina. We discussed the options at that time for teaching or pursuing secretary and nursing tracks. She did not decide on any of these choices immediately, but relocated to New York City to live with me and was employed by the New York Telephone Company. She simultaneously worked part-time on weekends as a unit clerk in a local hospital to get experience in a health care facility and to consider nursing school. One year later she decided to attend nursing school, graduated and had a successful 32-year career in nursing.

CHAPTER SIX

FAMILY CONCERNS

"Family life is full of major and minor crises - the ups and downs of health, success and failure in career, marriage, and divorce- and all kinds of characters. It is tied to places and events and histories. With all of these felt details, life etches itself into memory and personality. It's difficult to imagine anything more nourishing to the soul."

— Thomas Moore

There is great joy in having a healthy relationship with your family and tremendous fun in going on trips and attending positive family events such as celebrations, marriages, and births. But a challenge that we all face at some point are when bad times fall on them (and us). Most harsh are the illness and the deaths of family members. It is so hard for us to see our loved ones fall sick, suffer and leave us. It also makes very aware, as we get older, of our own mortality.

In spite of the many significant and positive events in my life with family, some deaths affected me profoundly. The loss of my brother, friend and mentor Dr. Jack Trowell who passed in July 1993. My father, Frank the "wheel man" in September 1998. My mother, Irene Battle the family matriarch in January 2008 and my brother Lee, my best friend and confidant in October 2009. For me, the final act of death cannot be accurately described psychologically in words.

While not to marginalize the pain of such events as death, stop and think a moment about those we love who have passed on. All their worries have now ceased. They have no suffering and no longer face earthly fears, and sure, they have left us all behind and we miss them so... but shedding tears is one of the things the living do. They have gone to a better life of happiness in a paradise and place we all have dreamed. Death leaves a heartache no one can heal and love leaves a memory no one can steal. We can recognize the importance of those closest to us that have passed on by honoring their memory and by taking care of the living. I believe that is how you cherish the memory of loved ones who have passed on.

Health History and Its Importance

No one escapes death. But there are things within our family experience that we learn can help us lead healthier lives. And certainly the knowledge can work in our favor when dealing with our health proactively to head off potential problems. We need to be aware of family medical history and tell members to seek preventive health measures and to take care of themselves. Due to many unusual family illnesses and deaths each year, I remind family members annually about family medical history based on interviews and research of death records. In reviewing my own family history (archival records) from 1836 to December 2013. I listed diseases and conditions prevalent in the Trowell, and more recent Battle (1900), family history and shared with my family. This data came from a review of death certificates, newspaper articles, recent deaths, state, and county vital statistical files.

Family members are advised to get annual physical examinations and more frequent evaluations if signs or symptoms occur associated with the listed conditions or diseases. Even though prevention is the key to avoiding some diseases or to lessen the severity of their impact, as we get older family illness history will still affect our health. Like the saying goes, "Forewarned is forewarned..." Take the time to learn about your family's medical history. That knowledge helps saves lives each year.

These are diseases and symptoms prevalent mainly in female ancestors including maternal mothers, grand and great-grandmothers, aunts, sisters, and cousins. Cancer: breast, uterine, kidney, and brain. Others such as arthritis, knee and hip problems, diabetes, osteoporosis, bursitis, high cholesterol, cataracts, nearsightedness, brain aneurysm, hypertension; psychological including depression, schizophrenia, and bipolar disorder.

These are diseases and symptoms prevalent mainly in male ancestors including paternal fathers, grand and great-grandfathers, uncles, brothers, and cousins. Primarily, and perhaps most deadly is Cancer: lung, colorectal, prostate with high PSA, leukemia, and pancreatic; others such as arthritis, diabetes, bursitis, heart disease, stroke, hypertension, nearsightedness, brain aneurysm and gout; psychological including depression and schizophrenia. In my own family, I had male members who suffered from Shell Shock (what we now call PTSD) from combat in WWII.

Other family health issues include dealing with mental health concerns and caring for elderly parents and other relatives. The key is to address issues quickly and with joint family assistance when possible, in consultation with health care providers and religious institutions. As we know (or you may come to experience), some family members do not assist or cooperate in supporting ill relatives. In spite of that and other challenges, do not allow tragedies to define your work and life. Do your very best and move forward by honoring the dead and also by supporting and taking care of the living. These are responsibilities you should never shirk.

Education & Careers

As a family practice, we encourage children to think about their career plans early in elementary school with continuous support through graduation from high school. I frequently talk with nieces, nephews and others about career options and choices. All high school graduates in our family are encouraged to attend college, technical school or other specialized training for career skills. Some family members elect to join the military or find jobs. However, many of do eventually seek admission to a university concurrent with their service in the military or employment.

An example of consultation with one niece: Karen, a nurse, was trying to decide what course of action to take pursuing a master's degree. We discussed the numerous options and reviewed data on which fields offered the most future opportunities. She considered clinical, legal, policy, health informatics and administrative tracks. She selected health informatics and graduated with a master's degree in that field.

We also encourage young family members to postpone marriage until graduating from college or achieving stability as an adult. I believe they will be more mature, better educated, and in a position to financially support a family. With affordable housing, health insurance, child care (and a plan for their children's education) recreation and vacation options are opportunities to explore and include as part of work life balance.

Just like with other families, sometimes younger family members may select a major in college but change course later to a different career path. As a support system, we assist them in obtaining scholarships, part-time jobs, mentors and stay in contact. I also ask them to network with each other and maintain family relationships.

During my generation, we helped family members financially to attend college, without expecting anything in return. We only desired that they become successful in a career of their choice. Many of our family members did their part and helped others by giving back and paying it forward for future generations.

People don't seem to help others as much as they used to years ago. If we had not assisted family members many years ago with college would we have all the successes noted in the family accomplishments section of this memoir or over the years? Probably not and if the help had not been given the outcome most likely would have been drastically different.

The family does not just end with parents and siblings, though. I've helped fourteen of my 32 nieces and nephews obtain scholarships and pay for college. At the family reunions, I helped organize every three years, I tell them to stay in touch, to keep their lives in balance and to keep learning. I advise them to turn obstacles into stepping stones and that persistence pays off. One story I share with them illustrates this. Early in my career in the Air National Guard, a chief nurse warned me that I'd never make it past Major, "no matter how good I was." I just thanked her and said, "Okay." She had her opinion but I didn't let it bother me. I went four ranks beyond what she said would be my limit, to Major General. That accomplishment is a better response than any I could ever have given her.

CHAPTER SEVEN

Family Accomplishments and Travel

"Family means no one gets left behind or forgotten."

— David Ogden Stiers

In spite of challenges, my family members have accomplished Herculean goals in their lives. 2013, 2014 and 2015 were banner years and I attended most of these events with family members. These included graduations, promotions and other accomplishments and events. A tremendous variety of successes from dedicated and brilliant family members, in spite of the economic and other challenges over the last few years! I just love graduations and promotions for anyone, but especially that of my family and friends, since they depict accomplishments and the honoring of individuals personally.

Accomplishments

April 2013: Ieshia Abney was elected 2012-2013 as Student Government Secretary at Aiken Technical College. Ieshia and the three other officers came up with a project called U-Knighted 4 Fitness. They won First Place against eight other South Carolina Technical Colleges and traveled to Myrtle Beach, South Carolina for the awards ceremony.

May 2013: Ieshia Abney graduated on May 7, 2013, from Aiken Technical College with an Associate of Arts degree. She also received an award for Outstanding Leadership and Service for Student Government Association as Secretary for the 2012-2013 school year. She is now working on her bachelor's degree.

May 2013: Elijah James Bell, III graduated from Harvard Medical School (MD) on May 30, 2013, and is currently training in Emergency Medicine at Baylor College of Medicine in Houston, Texas. He is the son of Shirley Trowell-Bell, MD.

July 2013: Joshua William Trowell received his Eagle Scout from Troop 1657. He is a college pre-med and Public Health student at the University of Maryland. He has received numerous letters of acknowledgment from senior leaders from Troop 1657, religious community, Congressional Legislators, state senators, county representatives, university professors, and President and Mrs. Obama.

July 2013: Karen Hankinson graduated with an M.S. in Health Informatics from Walden University. Using the knowledge gained but attaining this degree she will help improve the efficiency and quality of healthcare services. This effort will also contribute to reducing health care costs, increase patient access to care, improve the diagnosis, treatment, and outcomes of disease. This is a relatively new specialty area in health care, especially for electronic medical records.

August 2013: Crystal and Damian Jorge welcomed their son, Damian Andres on August 29, 2013.

September 2013: Joshua Trowell 16, a community health major, was one of seven diverse University of Maryland students who founded Public Health Without Borders to educate and serve communities in developing countries. The team has spent time on projects in Peru and Bangladesh, now in the summer of 2015 they visited Ethiopia.

October 2013: Dr. Elijah Bell, III published an article: Information Technology Improves Emergency Department Patient Discharge Instructions Completeness and Performance on a National Quality Measure.

October 2013: Demetrius Trowell became the Project Manager of the contracting web team for the Federal Highway Administration (FHWA).

November 2013: Donna Trowell Piotrowski retired from the Army National Guard on August 4, 2013, at the rank of Captain after 20 years and 4 months of service. She graduated from American Military University on November 15, 2013, with a Master's of Science Degree in Environmental Policy and Management.

December 2013: Jewel Trowell completed his MBA (Master of Business Administration) and is now working on his Doctorate in business administration.

These next three are children of Calvin and Altha Trowell - Durham, NC and are grandsons of Rev. Jacob Calvin Trowell and the late Mary Trowell of Augusta, GA.

December 2, 2013: eldest son Joseph Brian Trowell, age 22, a graduate of East Carolina University is an Assistant Construction Site Supervisor in Upper Marlboro, Maryland.

Joseph graduated with a degree in Construction Management and Minor in Business Administration.

Twin 1: Andre Jacob Trowell, age 21, Junior Summer School Student and Student Library Page at Appalachian State University. He is majoring in Health Care Management. He mentors others and is a part of several student auxiliary organizations services.

Twin 2: Charles Alexander Trowell, age 21, Junior University of North Carolina at Charlotte. He is an Architecture Major and was a summer 2014 Architectural Intern at the Capitol in Washington, DC.

Their Parents: Dad, Calvin Trowell, is working in the Engineering field and Mom, Altha Trowell is a teacher taking courses this year in Durham, NC.

February 2014: Selina Jorge a brilliant and accomplished 8-year old received three school awards: (1) Honor Roll for As and Bs, (2) Attendance, maintained one day or less absence during 2nd Quarter and (3) Personal Responsibility an unprecedented award.

February 25, 2014: Trevor Trowell released a DVD with fourteen videos**: The #MyFitLifeMixTape** to inspire and motivate others and focus on TreWell Fitness. Also, these videos show what consistency, commitment, and dedication does for an individual. This mixtape is a first of its kind fitness video mixtape where the artist's music and videos are put together with fitness videos to help create a vibe of excitement and inspiration by words and visual aid.

March 2014: Ravyn Hankinson was selected President of Student Government Association (SGA). Responsibilities of the individual, thereby developing an appreciation of membership in democracy. To develop good citizenship by giving the students an opportunity to have a part in self-government. To help with the coordination of extracurricular activities. To bring about a closer relationship between the students, faculty and administration. To encourage the development of school spirit through participation and to demand the best possible academic atmosphere. In keeping with these purposes, the SGA plays a significant role in helping to plan and coordinate the various student activities within the school. Rayvn graduated from high school June 2015 and will enter Radford University in the fall to study communications and social work.

May 3, 2014: Selina Jorge signed up and competed in the Capital Clubhouse Skating Academy "Glide Into Spring 2014" in the National Capital Area Competition Series. The competition is to display basic skills and usually is for skaters who have never taken private lessons.

May 2014: Jeremiah Harris son of Angeline Trowell-Harris graduated from high school and is now enrolled at Citadel in Charleston, South Carolina.

May 10, 2014: Brian Trowell graduated from the University of South Carolina in Columbia with a degree (BS) in Electrical Engineering with a minor in Computer Engineering. He now works as an engineer at a large company in Grantville, South Carolina.

May 18, 2014: Lori Rogers Belyea, daughter of Valda Trowell Lofton graduated from Tufts Medical School with her Doctor of Medicine (MD). She simultaneously graduated from Brandeis University with a Master of Business Administration (MBA).

June 6, 2014: Charlie Robert Abney Jr., graduated from Strom Thurmond High School and is now attending the University of South Carolina studying Communications and Sports Management. He is the son of Charlie and Jacqueline Trowell Abney.

June 9, 2014: Henry Lloyd celebrated his 90th birthday in Aiken, South Carolina with tons of cards and letters from family members and friends. He passed away March 2015.

October 11, 2014: Khadine and Demetrius held their baby shower.

October 14, 2014: Jessica Trowel published new artwork on Artsonia.com!

November 18, 2014: Khadine and Demetrius welcome their child, a daughter Zoe Ava, to the world!

February 28, 2015: Jessica Trowell has new artwork on Artsonia.com! Created by Jessica in Grade 11 at Oxon Hill High School. Part of a school project called "Deconstruction of a Cereal Box." Published on February 27 by Allison Richo (Jessica's teacher).

These were excellent accomplishments and I congratulate all family members for their individual successes!

But like many families, we have some so-called deadbeats and those that behave badly at times. All had numerous opportunities, but made excuses and did not pursue available employment or academic options. We are always working and encouraging them with the support of scholarships and other resources. However, they must help themselves first. Our goal is to change the family paradigm from low paying jobs to college level, better-paying leadership positions when possible.

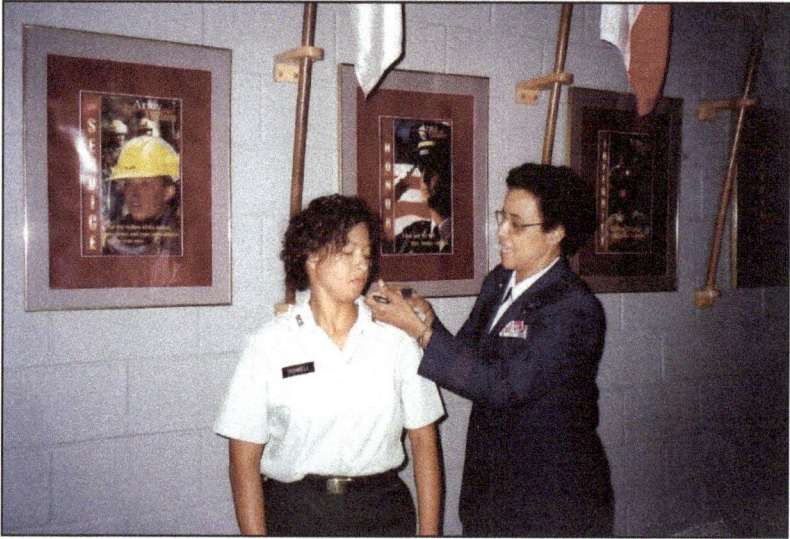

Maj. Gen. Trowell-Harris Pinning 2nd Lieutenant Bars on niece, Donna Trowell Protrowski, Army Reserve, 2002

I mentioned paying attention to saving funds, retirement planning and investing in the stock market or other methods to increase financial status. If I had not done this financial planning, in coordination with my broker and tax accountant, I would not have been able to assist family members financially:

- Sister with nursing school
- Brothers with medical school and pilot training
- On graduation from nursing school: I sent my parents monthly checks for 50 years
- Established the Endowed Leadership Fund at The American Nurses Foundation

- Support the Major General Irene Trowell-Harris Chapter of Tuskegee Airmen, Inc.
- Established the Irene Battle Trowell (mother) Memorial Education Fund with the Aiken County Historical Museum
- Support many other educational and charity initiatives

Travel

"Some have a gift for helping others to see the world as a place of possibility... Some impart wisdom or comfort and care. Some point out the path, and some take you there."

— Unknown

Early in my career I learned to enjoy travel and realize its benefits.

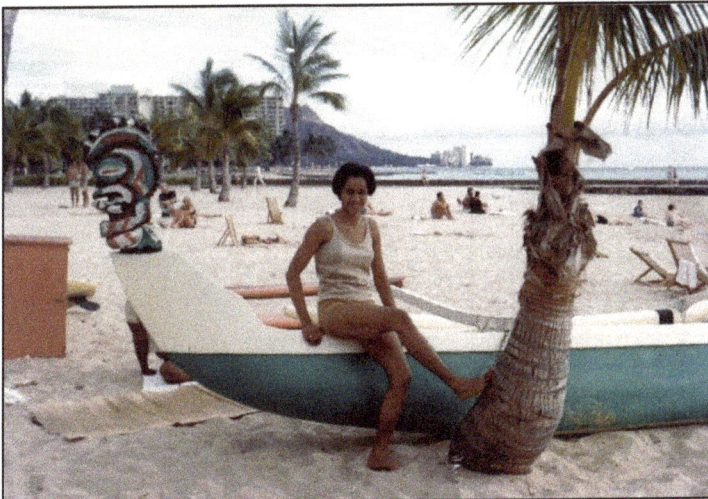

Beach, May 1967, Honolulu, Hawaii

It is a real joy working with family members and friends on various activities and festivities, including hosting family brunches, graduations, attending movies, plays, and operas. We also attend concerts mainly at Kennedy Center, Strathmore Theatre, and DAR Constitution Hall in Washington, DC. Since the 1960s, I have sponsored various family members at intervals to events such Radio City Christmas Spectacular show in NYC and the Albuquerque International Hot Air Balloon Festival. The family celebrates July 4 and Thanksgiving each year as a joint effort and team in Aiken, South Carolina. Each person prepares their favorite dish and shares with the larger group. We started taking family trips in the early 1970s traveling initially to Bermuda and Vienna, Austria. I've traveled a great deal in life and it is a joy to go to those places and new ones with family and friends. Over the past few years, family members enjoyed many trips and events such as:

- To Las Vegas and to see the Hoover Dam.
- Vacation cruises and a longer 10-day cruise to Europe in September 2008.
- My nephew's wedding in Cancun May 2008. What a beautiful moment for our family.
- My older sister and I spent eight days in Rome January 2009 visiting Vatican City, attending the Pope's New Year's Procession, visiting the Coliseum, touring other famous sites and shopping.
- Eight days in Paris, France in 2012 with two of my nieces. We visited the Eiffel Tower, Cathedral of Notre Dame, the Grand Louvre, and many other fascinating places.
- I visited Aruba, Dutch Caribbean in 2013 for 8 days with two nieces. It included an island survey tour, Palm Beach, Butterfly Farm, Natural Bridge and other beautiful sites.

- Other trips included Switzerland, Sweden, Norway and Denmark.

Perhaps the most significant to me spiritually was in September 2008. Five family members traveled with me for 12 days on a Holy Land cruise through Turkey, Greece and Italy tracing the steps of St. Paul.

The purpose of this trip was to gain greater insights into the writings of the apostle Paul through this Christian tour. We walked in the land where he preached, as both a captive and free man. All the while, taking in the beauty God has created as we cruised through the Greek Isles and explored the amazing ruins of ancient Roman strongholds in Turkey.

We enjoyed exploring the following cities: Athens, Thessaloniki, Veria, Kavala, Philippi, Istanbul, Dikili, Pergamon, Kusadasi, Ephesus, Miletus, Patmos, and Corinth. With each area presenting a unique aspect of history, culture and purpose:

- Thessaloniki - The house where Paul lived and the Agora where he preached
- Philippi - Home to the Baptistery of Lydia
- Istanbul - Topkapi Palace, Blue Mosque, and Hagia Sofia
- Mykonos - White-washed beauty
- Ephesus - The Great Amphitheater where Paul spoke to the Ephesians
- Patmos - The "Holy Island" where John wrote Revelation
- Rhodes - The oldest inhabited medieval town in Europe with its fortifications built by the Crusaders of St. John

- Crete - It was here that Paul left Titus to lead the church he started
- Athens - The Acropolis, Agora, and Mars Hill
- Corinth - Explored the ruins of the ancient Greek city where Paul worked including the Agora where he was on trial at the Bema

In June 2014, we went on another 12-day Historical Holy Land Cruise. The ship made stops in Istanbul, Turkey, Ephesus-Kusadasi, Turkey, Rhodes, Greece; Patmos, Greece, Limassol, Cyprus, Haifa, Israel and Athens (Piraeus), Greece.

This was a riveting journey. What we saw was history and culture with all the emotions of joy, comedy, beauty, awe, wonder, creativity, beauty that captured the human spirit, suffering and abject sadness of the Holocaust Museum. All our lifelong religious teaching and history are presented in thousands of years in art, music, knowledge, culture and stone structures.

There were many points of interest. The principal areas we visited during the cruise included the beautiful Sea of Galilee, the Mount of Olive; Jordan River (we washed our feet in the river), The Holocaust and Children's Museum; Nazareth, The Wailing Wall (now the West Wall), Jerusalem, and seaport of Haifa where our ship docked.

I visited Hong Kong, China 22-29 July 2014 to attend the Honor Society of Nursing, Sigma Theta Tau International 25th International Nursing Research Congress. The research sessions were most informative and valuable.

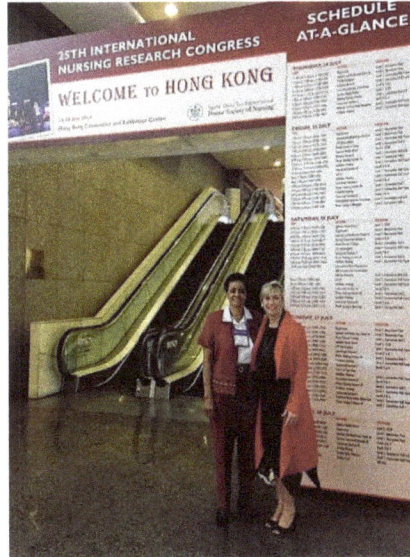

The 25th International Nursing Research Congress

Some highlights from a day's survey tour. A ride on the Victoria Peak tram, panoramic views from atop Victoria Peak, picturesque Repulse Bay, Aberdeen's floating community, shopping for bargains at Stanley Market and watching craftsmen at work in a well-known jewelry factory.

The sightseeing Hong Kong Night Cruise and Dinner with dancing were excellent. We experienced the magic of Hong Kong at night with an evening cruise on Hong Kong's dazzling Victoria Harbor, followed by an 8-course Chinese banquet at Aberdeen's famous Jumbo Floating Restaurant.

Other highlights included: the Hong Kong city light up during a 1.5-hour cruise aboard a traditional Chinese sightseeing boat while enjoying unlimited drinks served from the open bar during the cruise. We observed stunning night views of Hong Kong and Kowloon from the Mid-Levels lookout, halfway up Victoria Peak.

We also toured the Hong Kong Polytechnic University, a well-known university with training of nurses and paramedical staff, situated in front of the cross-harbor tunnel. The University highlighted its Integrative Health Clinic; Traditional Chinese Medicine Laboratory; and School of Nursing Laboratory including an acupuncture demonstration.

My most recent international trips, in 2015, were a Panama Canal cruise in March 2015, a trip to Seoul, South Korea to participate in the International Council of Nursing Summit 17-24 June and to San Juan, Puerto Rico in July.

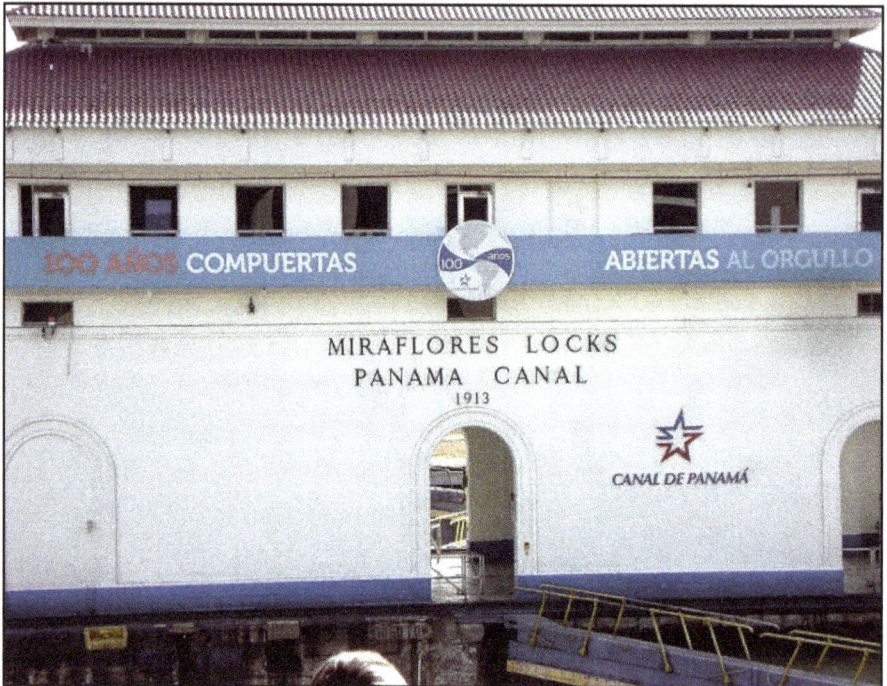

Panama Canal cruise March 2015

In the Panama Canal

In one of the locks of the Panama Canal

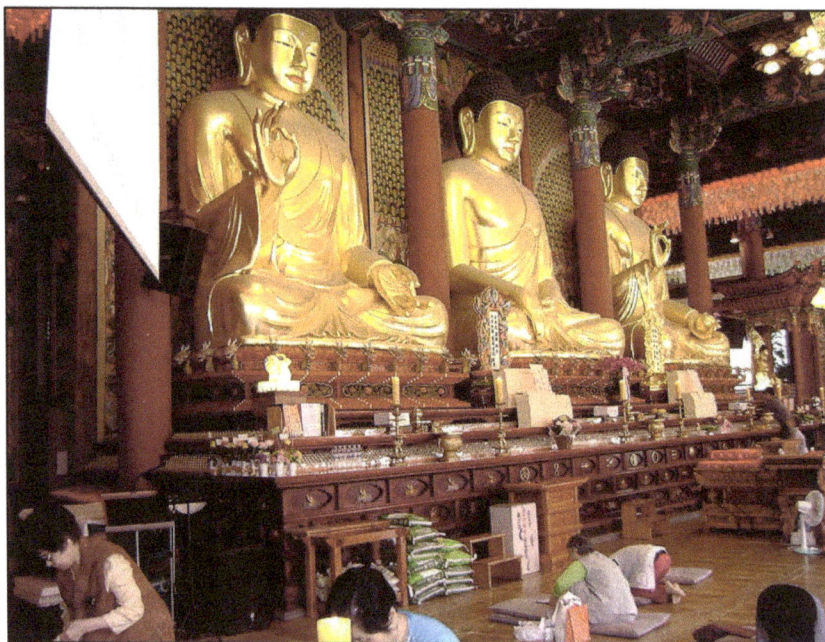

Photo in Shrine, Seoul, Republic of Korea

Photo in Seoul, in kimono

At Monument, Seoul

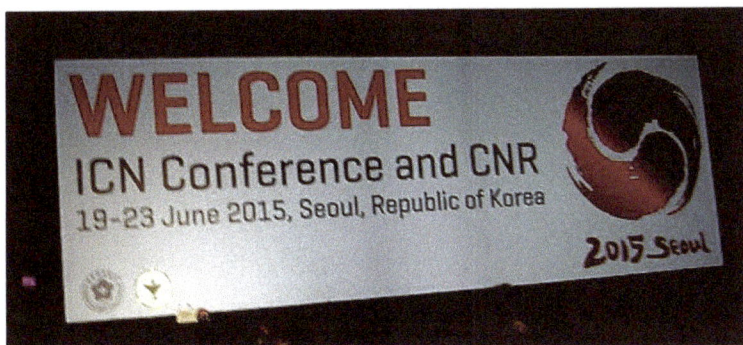

A Wonderful International Event

An Important Aspect of Travel

"How Ya Gonna Keep 'em Down on the Farm (After They've Seen Paree?)" is a World War I song that rose to popularity after the war had ended. The lyrics highlight the concern that American soldiers from rural environments would not want to return to farm life after experiencing the European city life and culture of Paris during World War I.

I, like countless millions of Americans over the centuries our nation has existed, was born and raised in a rural environment. It can be, and in many ways was, an excellent place to grow up. And a rural setting is still the choice of many to stay beyond childhood to adulthood; to raise families. And it may also become a final resting place. But I know that once I left home I was changed forever. I became a much different person that if I had never left. And in my opinion it made me a better person for having seen, experienced and come to love the different places I've had the opportunity to travel to.

Above I wrote about being able to treat family members to travel and memorable experiences. They enjoyed them tremendously and still talk about them today. To watch them and see the look in their eyes as they visited the Eiffel Tower, Notre Dame, and the Louvre Museum—that is perhaps the greatest gift I can be given. I've been blessed with rewards for the hard work in my life. It warmed my heart to be able to see the younger generation of family members see firsthand how wonderful our world is. It delighted me to see them enjoy the splendors of cities and cultures many centuries older than what we experience here in the United States. And I know, as travel and new places had their impact on me, that these trips and memories from them will have a ripple effect. They will continue to have an impact on those who I have had the tremendous pleasure to travel with.

*"I felt my lungs inflate with the onrush of scenery—
air, mountains, trees, people. I thought, "This is what
it is to be happy."*

— Sylvia Plath, the Bell Jar

I have been blessed, in my travels, to have many of those moments in life. A scene, a place, a perfect moment that you felt deep inside. And it filled you with wonder at how beautiful our world is, how vast its history, the unique people and places and how special it was to be there. For the young person(s) who read this; I recommend you travel as often as you can once you've secured the basic necessities for life and for your future. Plan and budget for those things but also, if you can, allow time for travel. I firmly believe the experience you gain from it is a force (and joy) multiplier in your life.

Something I Recommend If You Travel Often

Due to my frequent national and international travel, I applied for and received the TSA Pre-Check and the Global Entry Card to avoid long lines at airports. TSA Pre√™ allows low-risk travelers to experience faster, more efficient screening at participating United States airport checkpoints for domestic and international travel. Once approved, passengers receive a Known Traveler Number (KTN) which is embedded in the barcode of future boarding passes with TSA Pre√™ also printed on the front of boarding passes.

Those who are approved for the global entry program can re-enter the US by using a kiosk at an airport to get authorization to re-enter the US. The kiosk reads the traveler's passport or green card. The screen of the kiosk is used as a fingerprint scanner to verify identity. At the kiosk, the traveler is asked whether they have anything to declare at customs. Once the session is complete, usually in just a few minutes, the machine prints a transaction receipt and the traveler can then exit the airport or claim their baggage and then exit. This is much faster than having to go through customs each time and frees up United States Customs and Border Protection authorities to focus on higher-risk passengers. This can actually help enhance safety for everyone.

PART 3

THE PRESENT & FUTURE

"No matter how busy you are, you must take the time to make the other person feel important."

— Mary Kay Ash, American businesswoman

CHAPTER EIGHT

RETIREMENT & PAYING IT FORWARD

"As we look ahead into the next century, leaders will be those who empower others."

— Bill Gates

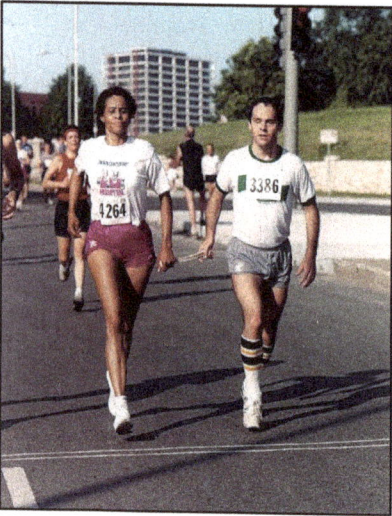

Hospital Hill Run with Blind Colleague, 1987 - Kansas City

From the beginning of my career, I helped others along the way in nursing, in the Air Force and Air National Guard, at church, and in my community.

In all the walks of my life: civilian, military and federal arenas. I worked on many institutional scholarships and endowments to help educate the next generation. I have consistently donated to various institutions that touched my life. Including: Mount Hill Missionary Community Church, Jersey City State University, Yale, Columbia, Aiken County Historical Museum, Columbia Hospital School of Nursing, American Nurses Association (ANA), American Nurse Foundation donations for leadership and African-American research, Women's Memorial, American Red Cross, now the Dr. Irene Trowell-Harris Endowed Leadership Fund and also the Major General Irene Trowell-Harris Chapter of Tuskegee Airmen, Inc. (www.tai-ny.org).

With my retirement from federal service on September 30, 2013, I began devoting time to various institutions and exploring academic scholarships for students to help educate the next generation of leaders. Another goal I have is to continue to honor veterans, by assisting some museums in collecting history memorabilia—including Women's Memorial, my hometown museum, Aiken County Historical Museum, where my military photo and Yale alumni chair are both on display.

All of these organizations are important. However, I wish to briefly discuss Women in Military Service for America Foundation (WIMSA) since it is the only museum that represents all women, all services, and all eras. I am a charter member of WIMSA; a wall plaque was given for supporting military service members and veterans, consistent donations and my accomplishment as a military officer. The plaque with name was placed in the Hall of Honors, 2005. Currently, I am a member of the WIMSA Leadership Circle addressing long-term plans for the museum. The foundation has registered over 250,000 of the two million women eligible to register.

The Women's Memorial:

- recognizes all women who have served in or with the United States Armed Forces—the past, present, and future;
- documents the experiences of these women and tells their stories of service, sacrifice, and achievement;
- makes their contributions a visible part of our history;
- illustrates their partnership with men in defense of our nation, and
- serves as inspiration for others.

I am giving back to the major institutions that touched my life, inspired, helped, mentored and offered me a galaxy of opportunities to become successful. There is no greater way of showing my appreciation than to help those institutions help others as they helped me.

When I was young, I developed a guide for daily living based on my religious foundation and extensive military education and training. Below are those general principles that I used daily for decision making throughout my life and career.

- Always be respectful of others.
- Do not wish to solve world hunger, but help make changes personally and professionally within my circle of influence and control.
- Use what you have – don't wait for perfection, but strive for excellence.
- Did not want or expect anything in return from others personally for helping or mentoring, however, ask them to help others when opportunities present themselves.
- Do not take things personal and always pick your battles (first making sure it is something battle-worthy).
- Connect with people for collaboration through networking and sharing.
- Make the best decision based on the facts you have at that time.
- Embrace physical fitness, positive health behavior and maintain balance in life.
- Honor the dead by taking care of the living.
- Place items in the Mental Parking Lot to be dealt with at a later date. This included difficult items waiting for the right time and support.

These general principles have served me well throughout my life and career and are still used during retirement.

Giving Back and Paying It Forward Helping Others

"Wherever there is a human being, there is an opportunity for a kindness."

— Seneca, Roman philosopher

Public service is a commitment to honoring the importance of ensuring the well-being of others; it is a dedication to helping our fellow Americans. And I believe in giving back to others to benefit the community, state, and country. Inspiring and mentoring others extend beyond my individual aspirations. I did not want or expect anything in return from others personally for helping or mentoring, however, I ask them to help others when opportunities present themselves. Investment in the human potential stock market provides benefits for a lifetime.

Giving back is an investment in the future by helping young people reach their career goals, just like the various institutions invested in me to help me become successful. The church served as the foundation that guided me throughout my personal life and professional career and served as the bridge from the cotton field to the nursing school.

My question for giving back and paying forward is: how do we inspire others to give back? Not just family members and friends, but those we meet every day at work, in school, religious services, community events and other locations. Giving back could be in many forms, not just financially, but for example: by mentoring, donating blood, volunteering at agencies that support youth or the elderly, education, food banks and other causes. Next question. Why not invest in the human potential stock market just like we invest in the stock market for financial benefit? Both of these investments can provide benefits for a lifetime. Just thank Yale and Columbia University invested in me by providing financial support for a master's and doctorate degrees.

In December 2013, I established the American Nurses Foundation (ANF) Irene Trowell-Harris Endowed Leadership Fund.

American Nurses Foundation
IRENE TROWELL-HARRIS
ENDOWED LEADERSHIP FUND

AGREEMENT is made this 11th day of December, 2013, by and between Irene Trowell-Harris, (the "Donor") and the ANF, a nonprofit District of Columbia corporation, (the "Foundation").

WHEREAS, the Donor desires to establish, and the Foundation is willing to hold and administer, a charitable fund (the "Fund") for the purpose of supporting the leadership development of nurses – with special focus on those serving or having served in the military and in non-traditional nursing roles. The aim of the fund is to support leadership development of nurses – especially those with military experience and in non-traditional roles, which is in furtherance of the educational and other charitable purposes of the Foundation.

The ANF is the charitable and philanthropic arm of the American Nurses Association (ANA), the only full-service professional organization representing the interests of the nation's 3.4 million registered nurses through its constituent and state nurses associations and its organizational affiliates. The Foundation supports programs that transform the nation's health through the power of nursing.

CHAPTER NINE

MAJOR PROJECTS AND ACTIVITIES

"You are never too old to set another goal or to dream a new dream."

— C. S. Lewis

My first book, (*Sky High: No Goal is Out of Your Reach*, Adducent, Veterans Publishing Systems 2010) was written as an inspirational tool to motivate others to success, and to encourage young people to stay in school and apply themselves academically. It is also for those who are stuck-in-place and need a little encouragement to jump-start their careers. This memoir includes new details about my life not covered in that book.

I am also working on selected veterans' projects on history and reintegration. Recently I served as moderator for a Georgetown University forum on that focused on military, veteran and family member reintegration.

New Adventures and Future Plans

This section includes some items from my bucket list. What are the next challenges for me, now that I am retired?

- First, is to stay healthy mentally and physically and engaged in meaningful activities and projects.

- Then to continue national and international travel with family members.

- To increase my time working with various institutions, and exploring academic scholarships for low-income students.

- To keep honoring veterans by serving those who have served our country.

- To continue to serve on advisory councils and committees such as Code of Support, WIMSA, and TAI Foundation Board.

- You're reading one of them that I've accomplished: completing another book–a memoir. My first book was written to inspire young people to apply themselves academically and to stay in school. This time I would like to focus on sharing my life's journey and the lessons I learned along the way.

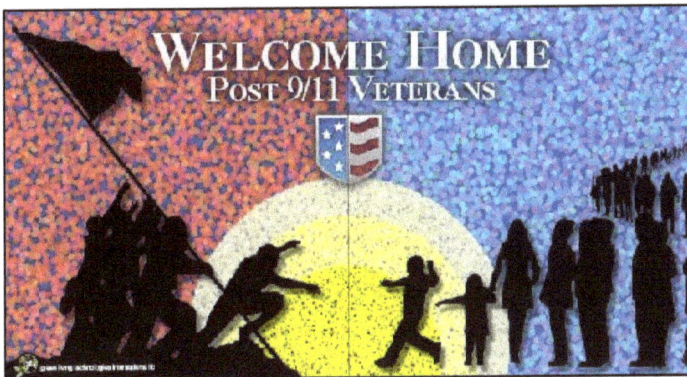

Code of Support, "Living Wall of Honor,"
WWII Memorial, August 2014

A new, unexpected opportunity came up in 2014. I was asked to serve as moderator for a Veterans event (sponsored by Georgetown University, Dr. Kathy Kretman, Director, Center for Public and Nonprofit Leadership and Research Professor, McCourt

School of Public Policy). The event was held on March 21, 2014, at the Women in Military Service for America Memorial (WIMSA) at Arlington Cemetery. The forum and description follows.

Public Issue Forum: From Nation Building to Community Building and Capitalizing on The Strength of Our Veterans Here at Home

As United States forces presence in war zones is reduced, and the military is drawing down, increasing numbers of talented veterans and their families are returning to communities across the nation. Communities that sorely need the skills, creativity and leadership that our veterans have to offer. This event brings together a panel of renowned national and local leaders, veterans, and civilians, to discuss efforts underway across communities and sectors to reintegrate and engage veterans in the life and work of our communities.

This model will be used for universities and agencies nationally to help veterans and family members with education, employment, and other services.

Activities Since Retirement

These are some of the major activities since September 2013, not an all-inclusive list.

September 2013: Retired on September 30, 2013, from Federal service (SES) as a White House political appointee at VA after serving 25 years. Also, served over 38 years in the Air Force and Air National Guard.

October 18-20, 2013: Vacation to Aruba with Karen Hankinson and Sonya Bookard, nieces.

October 11, 2013: Attended Yale Alumni Day "Innovations in Public Health: A Homecoming" with Luncheon and Awards Ceremony, Yale School of Epidemiology, and Public Health, New Haven, Conn.

October 16, 2013: Attended the America Nurses Foundation, Friends of the National Institute of Nursing Research 2013 Gala, to honor research nurses at the Hyatt Regency Hotel on Capitol Hill, Washington, DC.

November 12, 2013: Attended the Teachers College, Columbia University 125th Anniversary Gala, "Celebrating a Tradition for Tomorrow," Apollo Theater, NYC. The purpose of the event was to benefit student scholarships at Teachers College.

December 2013: Established a Leadership Fund at the American Nurses Foundation (ANF) recognizing nurses in various areas including the military, Federal service and civilian/private sectors working in conjunction with ANA Advocacy Institute. The purpose of the Fund is to support leadership development of nurses – especially those with military experience and in non-traditional roles. There are 3.4 million nurses in the United States, but there will a shortage of 1.2 million in 2020 (IOM Report).

December 18, 2013: Major General Irene Trowell-Harris, United States Air Force (Ret.) with three others represented the Business and Professional Women's Foundation at The NBC Universal Foundation, in partnership with the NBC Universal Owned Television Stations. $1.2 million in grants was provided in ten markets for local nonprofit organizations including Business and Professional Women's Foundation, which received a $25,000 grant for its work with women who have served our country, including women veterans, military/veteran spouses and caregivers of wounded warriors. NBC 4 Featured BPW Foundation and Joining Forces Mentoring Plus.

February 1, 2014: Attended the MG Irene Trowell-Harris Chapter Tuskegee Airmen, Inc., 16th Annual Tuition Assistance Awards Celebration, "Climb High, Dream Higher... Attitude Determines Altitude" at Anthony's Pier 9 in Newburgh, New York. The chapter honored and awarded scholarships to twelve students during the event.

February 21-24, 2014: Attended and supported the TAI Historical event to honor the original Tuskegee Airmen and their family members. The event also raised funds for student scholarships at the University of California, Riverside, CA.

March 14, 2014: Served as host for Retirement Ceremony of MSgt Angela Smith-Anderson, USAF at Sheppard Hall Conference Center, Air National Guard Readiness Center, Joint Base Andrews, Maryland.

March 21, 2014: Moderated a veteran's event at the Women in Military Service for America Memorial (WIMSA) at Arlington Cemetery sponsored by Georgetown University, Dr. Kathy Kretman, Director' Center for Public and Nonprofit Leadership and Research Professor, McCourt School of Public Policy. The 2014 Public Issue Forum was entitled "From Nation-Building to Community-Building: Capitalizing on The Strength of Our Veterans Here at Home."

April 9, 2014: Presented an educational session on "My Riveting Journey: A Life in Nursing, the Military, and Government Service as a White House Appointee," at New Jersey City University to faculty, students and employees, New Jersey.

April 12, 2014: Participated on a Leadership Panel "When Women Take the Lead" with Dr. Susan H. Fuhrman, President Teachers College, Columbia University at the 2014 Academic Festival in NYC.

April 25, 2014: Attended the 2014 AFNC Senior Lamp Briefings, Office of the Air Force Surgeon General, Medical development Facility, Fall Church, VA.

May 15, 2014: Received an honorary doctor of humane letters degree and then delivered remarks. She triumphed over adversity on many fronts, became a national advocate for women, diversity, and equal opportunity in both the military and civilian life. Dr. Trowell-Harris previously received an Honorary Doctorate of Humane Letters from the Medical College of Charleston. She is a Distinguished Alumni of Yale, Columbia, and NJCU.

May 21, 2014: Attended and marched in the Alumni Teachers College, Columbia University, Doctoral Hooding Convocation and Ceremony at the Cathedral of Saint John the Divine, NYC.

June 9-20, 2014: Went on a Historic Holy Land Cruise, Greece, Turkey, Cyprus and Israel for 12 days with niece Monica Perry and friends.

July 22-29, 2014: Attended the Sigma Theta Tau 25th International Nursing Research Congress in Hong Kong, China. The theme was "Engaging Colleagues: Global Health Outcomes."

September 11, 2014: Officiated event with Brigadier General Wilma Vaught, USAF (Retired) at the Code of Support Foundation (COSP) "Living Wall of Honor" dedication at WIMSA for the 160 military women who died in Iraqi and in Afghanistan. The COSP in partnership with the Women in Military Service to America Memorial Foundation, held a special ceremony to pay tribute to the women service members who have lost their lives in support of the wars in Afghanistan and Iraq since 9/11.

September 17, 2014: Honored as "Alumna of the Year for 2014" at the Columbia Hospital School of Nurses 17th Annual Alumni

Association Reunion "Celebrating Our Nursing History" in Columbia, South Carolina.

September 19, 2014: Attended the Yale University Alumni Day "The Affordable Care Act" with Luncheon and Awards Ceremony, New Haven Lawn Club, Conn.

October 4, 2014: Keynote speaker at the National Council Negro Women, Inc. Connecticut Sections, "Honoring Military Women of Color" Hartford Windsor Marriott Hotel, Windsor, Conn.

October 15, 2014: Attended the Friends of the National Institute of Nursing Research 2014 Gala," Expanding Nursing's Footprint in High Impact Research," Omni Shoreham Hotel, Washington, DC.

October 16-19, 2014: Attended the "Inspiring Global Leadership in the 211st Century" Summit at Yale University, New Haven, CT and spoke on 17 October at the Careers in Public Health Alumni Speaker Series on her "Life Story and Opportunities in Public Health" at the Yale University School of Epidemiology and Public Health.

October 26, 2014: Attended the 23rd Annual 2014 Fall Gathering Dinner Gala "Honoring the Valor, Courage and Sacrifice of Veterans," at the Army and Navy Country Club, Arlington, VA.

November 10, 2014: Honored by Business and Professional Women's (BPW) Foundation with five other outstanding military/veteran businesswomen and the employers who support them. NBWW awards are given in honor of these courageous and creative women and organizations who are making a difference in their military/veteran communities. The event was held at WIMSA and Mrs. Michelle Obama was the keynote, speaker.

November 11, 2014: Attended Women Veterans Rock Event, "Five Star Tribute to America's Women Veterans in Military

Service," and introduced and presented award to Cathie Lechareas as the "2015 Woman Veteran of the Year," at WIMSA.

November 13, 2014: Attended the Congressional Breakfast, "Returning Home: Challenges Facing Women Veterans Following Deployment" Rayburn House Office Building, DC, sponsored by Women's Policy, Inc., Disabled American Veterans and Women's Research and Education Institute in cooperation with Women in the Military/Veterans Task Force, Congressional Caucus for Women's Issues.

November 19, 2014: Presented at the VA Center for Women Veterans 20th Anniversary Celebration at the Department of Veterans Affairs on "Implementing the Vision for the Center for Women Veterans," HQ VACO, Sonny" Montgomery Veterans Conference Center, Washington, DC..

May 23, 2015: Served as Grand Marshall for Memorial Day Parade with the theme "A Grateful Aiken County Thanks and Honors You" in Aiken, South Carolina.

May 28, 2015: Honored and recognized with a medal as a "First" for 2015" by V-WISE, Syracuse University, The first female and nurse to command a medical clinic and first African-American woman in the history of the National Guard (357-year history of the National Guard) to be promoted to General Officer. In addition, the first to have a mentoring award and a Tuskegee Airmen, Inc., Chapter named in her honor.

June 8, 2015: Presented as keynote speaker at the Webb House, Inc. in Gary, Indiana. The program theme was "Celebration of Life." Over 200 women and men veterans attended the event. Webb House, Inc. is a nonprofit corporation that has pledged to provide safe housing, substance abuse counseling, employment assistance, and case management for our homeless veterans as they reintegrate into society. The agency is a community-based organization that strongly believes in the military commitment to assist our veterans and never leave a veteran behind.

June 17-24, 2015: Attended the International Council of Nurses (ICN) Conference in Seoul, The Republic of Korea. There were over 12,000 nurses from 132 countries sharing knowledge, policy, education and leadership across specialties, cultures and countries to help improve access and quality of care. This was an exceptional global networking experience. This international gathering of thousands of nurses explored the importance of cross-cultural understanding and global cooperation in nursing. The Conference provided opportunities for nurses to build relationships and to disseminate nursing knowledge and leadership across specialties, cultures, and countries. The three ICN pillars – Professional Practice, Regulation, and Socio-Economic Welfare – framed the scientific program and the dynamic exchange of experiences and expertise.

The International Council of Nurses (ICN) is a federation of more than 130 national nurses associations representing the millions of nurses worldwide. Operated by nurses and leading nursing internationally, ICN works to ensure quality nursing care for all and sound health policies globally.

July 23-27, 2015: Attended the Honor Society of Nursing, Sigma Theta Tau International (STTI) 26th International Nursing Research Congress in San Juan, Puerto Rico. Nearly 900 nurse leaders attended the Congress representing more than thirty countries with an opportunity to network with colleagues from around globe. The mission of the Honor Society of Nursing, Sigma Theta Tau International, is advancing world health and celebrating nursing excellence in scholarship, leadership, and service. This year's Congress theme was "Question Locally, Engage Regionally,

Apply Globally." The objectives of the Congress included (1) stimulate a global exchange of advanced practice nursing knowledge; (2) apply innovative nursing research outcomes; and (3) recognize the importance of nursing research discoveries in influencing practice, education, research, and health care policy. STTI's research priorities are advancing healthy communities through health promotion; preventing disease and recognizing social, economic, and political determinants; implementing evidence-based practice; targeting the needs of vulnerable populations such as the chronically ill and poor; and developing nurses' capacity for research.

Teachers College, Columbia University
Distinguished Alumni, 2005

EPILOGUE   IN CLOSING

"If you're trying to achieve, there will be roadblocks. I've had them; everybody has had them. But obstacles don't have to stop you. If you run into a wall, don't turn around and give up. Figure out how to climb it, go through it, or work around it."

— Michael Jordan

With the cherry blossoms in Washington DC, 2009

Now it is time to celebrate the life that I have lived, the discoveries I have made and the challenges I have met. But there are new ventures to be achieved. I have presented some key events of my life and career by decades beginning in the mid-1950s prior to completing high school and extending to 2014.

These key time points and events depict the challenges I've encountered and what I've done with my life. I know that I had a lot of help along the way from the places I've studied and learned, churches I've attended and worshiped at... and the many people that moved into my life that helped me when I needed it the most. This is the time to address a wonderful retirement with a bucket list and a sheet of music playing new ventures and initiatives.

I am giving back to the major institutions that touched my life, inspired, helped, mentored and offered me a galaxy of opportunities to become successful. Giving back is an investment in the future by helping young people reach their career goals, just like the various institutions invested in me to help me become successful. The church served as the foundation that guided me throughout my personal life and professional career. The church served as the bridge from the cotton field to nursing school and my faith help propelled me to unthinkable accomplishments.

Some Final Advice for a Productive and Enjoyable Life

- Develop a guide to general principles of daily living based on your religious foundation, life philosophy, education, and experience. I suggest that you use that to reflect daily on your decision making throughout your life and career.

- Ensure as you progress in your career, that you carefully plan for your retirement. Focus on various programs such as TSP, federal programs (FERS and CSRS), civilian pensions, military retirement, social security, and the stock market. The purpose of this is to ensure a comfortable life as a retiree and doing the things you always desired including national and international travel.

- Pick your battles and deal with issues that you can influence or solve. Do not try to solve world hunger, but help make changes personally and professionally within your circle of influence and control.

- Work on challenging issues by focusing on the facts and goals, not a political party. Use collaboration and coordination for project success.

- Embrace your family values and history. Always support and encourage youth to attend college, respect the wisdom of and care for the elderly, host and participate in family events such as graduations, weddings, family reunions, vacation trips, brunches for special occasions, recreation and theater events.

- Re-evaluate your career at intervals: think about where you are today, where you would like to be and what plans you have made to reach your dreams and goals. You may need to reshape or rebuild your life and career based on past choices if they have not yielded the results you want.

- Face reality. We plan for marriage, childbirth, college, employment, health, and life insurance and make wills. So let's make the final plan for death. Have specific plans for burial in writing and inform family members. This should include but is not limited to: insurance policy information, military protocol, location of burial, requests for specific such as type coffin (if desired), flowers, obituary information, clothing and any other requests. Usually, protocol for military service members for the rank of colonel and higher depending on service to include coffin in a caisson escorted with platoons, a band, and a rider-less horse.

- Continue to contribute (where you can make a difference) in spite of national and international challenges and negativity. Commit to helping resolve the many issues our country, and the world faces. Do great things and enjoy this country's beauty: parks, beaches, and notorious sites.

- In retirement stay focused, but willing to turn aside to help someone in need; move ahead, but not so fast that you can not smell the flowers. And take a bow, but applaud those who had a part in your success.

- In retirement, maintain a balanced diet and regular exercise. Stay healthy mentally and physically while being engaged in meaningful activities and projects.

- Enjoy life.

As I get older, I've realized that it's the relationships we develop that add depth to our personal and professional life. There are many people that have lives that span a continuum of contacts and transactional one-and-done events or experiences. Those are a component and part of everyone's life. But I can't imagine having a life that is completely like that. One that is a long thin line and a mere thread. To borrow an analogy from my friends that are veterans of the United States Navy, I prefer a strong mooring line.

I think many people—at least I know I do—get the most enjoyment and value out of things that are more than one layer deep. It could be the richness of a color (like one you feel you could dip your finger in). The texture of fine wood and look and feel of its grain. The savor of the food or drink, the subtleties and nuances of a well-written book, well-scripted, well-written movie or TV show. The pleasure of an intelligent discussion and conversation. The joy of visiting a new place and being able to have time to see beyond just the scenery.

It's the same for me when it comes to the quality of interaction other people. I hope that we all appreciate the special moment(s), appreciate the person... appreciate the truly valuable things we have and experience in life. They are what moor us in this world. As long as I have lived and as much as has been achieved personally and professionally each day I envision new ventures and receive new opportunities to contribute and excel.

"You are never too old to set another goal or to dream a new dream."

— C. S. Lewis

As a young child, I believed in faith, faith in God and in myself. Those simple beliefs built on the foundation of what my parents instilled in me—that I believe in still to this day—have carried me a very long way from my roots in South Carolina. And there's no better way to leave you than with this about success. Emerson had this right about what real success is!

To laugh often and much,
to win the respect of intelligent people and
the affection of children,
to earn the appreciation of honest critics and
endure the betrayal of false friends,
to appreciate beauty,
to find the best in others,
to leave the world a bit better,
whether by a healthy child, a garden patch...
to know even one life has breathed easier because
you have lived.
This Is to Have Succeeded!

— Ralph Waldo Emerson

Major Accomplishments

- Columbia Hospital School of Nursing Alumni Association Recognition as Nurse of the Year for 2014.

- Yale University - Masters in Public Health, 1973.

- Placed in the Yale University School of Medicine Honor Roll for dedication to public service, 2001.

- Distinguished Alumni of Yale University, 2006.

- Presented with a Distinguished Alumni Chair, 2006 (in Aiken County Historical Museum).

- Teachers College, Columbia University 2nd Masters' and Doctorate in Health Education, 1983.

- Distinguished Alumni of Columbia University, 2005.

- Inducted in Columbia University Nursing Hall of Fame, 1995.

- A graduate scholarship named in honor for academic years 2012 and 2014 (Major General Irene Trowell-Harris graduate scholarship).

- New Jersey City University, Bachelor's Degree in Health Education, 1971:

- Distinguished Alumni of New Jersey City University, 2014.

- Honorary Degree, Doctor of Humane Letters, NJCU May 2014.

- Honorary Degree, Doctor of Humane Letters from the Medical University of South Carolina, for outstanding achievements in the field of nursing, the military and the community, May 16, 1997.

- First African-American female in National Guard history to be promoted to General Officer rank, 1993. Photo in Pentagon, on the African-American Corridor.

- Promotion to the rank of Major General (2-stars) in the United States Air Force and Air National Guard,1998.

- Tuskegee Airmen, Inc. chapter named her in honor - Major General Irene Trowell-Harris Chapter of Tuskegee Airmen, Inc., Newburgh, New York. First female in history to have a chapter named in her honor, 1999.

- Community Mentoring Award, named in honor by the ANG 105th Airlift Wing, Newburgh, New York. Given to an outstanding community person annually, 1999. The Military (New York Air National Guard) 105th Airlift Wing, Stewart ANG Base, Newburgh, NY named a mentoring award in my honor due to my lifelong mentoring of others, especially military members. The award is given annually to an outstanding community professional for mentoring at the Maj Gen Irene Trowell-Harris Chapter of Tuskegee Airmen, Inc. Last awarded 7 February 2015.

- Selected for the third annual Dr. James Weaver Society Award, for contribution to the military, 2002. The award was named in honor of Dr. Weaver; A distinguished Pennsylvania Congressman and Air National Guard Flight Surgeon.

- Retired from the United States Air Force/Air National Guard, September 30, 2001. Served over 38 years, attained the rank of Major General (2 stars); was awarded the Air Force Distinguished Service, Legion of Merit and New York State Conspicuous Service medals. Numerous Military Decorations and Citations (see service bio).

- Honored by the Dr. Mae Jemison Foundation of Excellence (Astronaut) for contributions to aviation and mentoring, October 6, 2006.

- Embry-Riddle Aeronautical University, Eagle of Aviation Award for mentoring, 2006.

- Selected by Women's eNews, NYC as one of "21 Leaders for the 21st Century for 2006" in the category of "Seven Who Construct New Realities."

- Honored by the Bessie Coleman Foundation for military achievements, support of aviation and mentoring, August 4, 2006.

Recognition

- Represented VA at the DACOWITS 2001-13 and White House Council on Women and Girls 2008-13.

- Certificate from Brookings Institution Executive Education, "Certification in Public Leadership," March 2010, Washington, DC.

- Certificate from Brookings Institution Executive Education, "The Executive Summit," March 16-18, 2010, St. Michaels, MD.

- Certificate from Brookings Institution Executive Education, "Leading with Integrity: Ethics in Action," March 1-3, 2010, Washington, DC.

- Secretary's Certificate of Recognition as a graduate of the VA Executive Fellows Program (2008-09) in conjunction with Brookings Institute, March 2009.

- Presented keynote speeches nationally and internationally on: legislation, women Veterans issues, leadership, team building, mentoring, educational opportunities, health care issues, women's benefits and services to numerous organizations: Congress, White House, University, political, federal, state, private; youth, VSOs, non-governmental agencies, women's and minority groups and other stakeholders.

- Charter member of the Women's Memorial (WIMSA), Arlington National Cemetery; a plaque with name placed in the Hall of Honors, 2005.

- Assistant Professor (Adjunct), Graduate School, Uniformed Services University of Health Services, Bethesda, MD, July 1990 to present.

- 1997 Air Force representative for the Committee on Women in the NATO Forces Conference held in Istanbul, Turkey and speaker for the Air Force in Pretoria, South Africa at an International Women's Conference.

- Established a scholarship in mother's memory in 2008 at the Aiken County Historical Museum to educate students of Aiken in history, especially military members and Veterans.

- December 2013 established the Dr. Irene Trowell-Harris Endowed Leadership Fund at the American Nurses

Foundation. The purpose of the Fund is to support leadership development of nurses especially those with military experience and in non-traditional roles.

- Active committee and member of numerous professional organizations including: MOAA, Business Professional Women, Kappa Delta Pi Honor Society, SES Association, Code of Support (Board of Directors), ANA, APHA, American Legion, WIMSA Senior Leadership Circle, NAACP, American Association of University Women, Honor Society of Nursing, Sigma Theta Tau International and AMSUS.

Major Publications

- Trowell-Harris, I. *Sky High: No Goal is Out of Your Reach*, Adducent: Veterans Publishing System, an imprint from Adducent, Jacksonville, FL, 2010.

- Trowell-Harris, I. Book Chapter in *Leadership in Action: Principles Forged in the Crucible of Military Service Can Lead Corporate America Back to The Top*, EDUCATION: Rear Admiral Greg Slavonic, et al., Fortis, a nonfiction imprint from Adducent, Jacksonville, FL, 2010.

- Trowell-Harris, I and Manning, L. Book Chapter on "Historical Progression: History of VA Health Care, Benefit Initiatives, and Selected Legislation for Women Veterans" in, *Glimpses of the New Veteran*, by Alice Booher, et al.' Published January 2015.

- Trowell-Harris, Irene. Mentoring Guide for the Air National Guard: *How to Implement a Military Mentoring Program | Suggested Strategies & Best Practices*. A Human Resources Quality Board Initiative, Maj. Gen. Irene Trowell-Harris,

Chairman, Human Resources Quality Board, Published September 18, 1999.

- Trowell-Harris, Irene. Air National Nurse Corps History. Published July 1993, *Highlights in the History of Air National Guard Nursing*. ANG, Washington, DC.

Date/Year	Life Milestones and Important Events (not All-Inclusive)
1939	Birth Aiken, South Carolina.
1939 - 1956	Early Life and Schooling in Aiken, South Carolina.
8/1/1956	Mount Hill Baptist Church and Martha Schofield High School united to share their financial resources and provide a scholarship for nursing school.
8/1/1956	Admitted to a three-year nursing program, a segregated school in August 1956 at Columbia Hospital School of Nursing in Columbia, South Carolina.
1956	At nursing school in 1956, I met Juanita and Andrew Martin who became my adopted parents at school in Columbia, South Carolina.
1/1/1959	American Nurses Association, ANA is the only full-service professional organization representing the interests of the nation's 3.4 million registered nurses.
9/5/1959	Graduated from Nursing School, Diploma in Nursing, Registered Nurse (RN), Columbia Hospital School of Nursing, Columbia, SC, 1959
9/5/1959	Started working at Talmadge Hospital in Augusta, Georgia.
1960	New York State Nurses Association, foster high standards of nursing, promote the professional and educational advancement of nurses.
7/1/1960	In July 1960, I relocated from Augusta, Georgia to White Plains, New York to complete a 3-month post-graduate course in Psychiatric Nursing since black students did not get this practical experience as part of their 3-year nurses training in South Carolina.

Date/Year	Life Milestones and Important Events (not All-Inclusive)
1/1/1963	While working at New York Hospital in New York City, I met two nurses who were in the New York Air National Guard as flight nurses. They invited me to visit the Floyd Bennett Field Air National Guard Base and check out the opportunities to become a military Flight Nurse.
4/6/1963	Commissioned in the ANG 1963
10/1/1963	Basic Officers Course and Flight Nurse School, 10/63-3/64.
1963	Association of Military Surgeons of the United States, life members (now The Society Federal Health Care of Professionals) AMSUS helps advance the knowledge of healthcare and increase the effectiveness of its members.
5/1/1964	Military airplane crash in 1964 in Charleston, South Carolina.
5/1/1971	Bachelor of Arts (BA) in Health Education, New Jersey City University, Jersey City, NJ, 1971, Cum Laude.
1971	American Public Health Association, attends conventions, APHA works to advance the health of all people and all communities.
5/1/1973	Master of Public Health (MPH) in Public Health Administration, Yale University, New Haven, CT, 1973
1974-1985	Nurse Consultant and Coordinator, January 1974 to July 1985 Departments of Nursing and Psychiatry, Our Lady of Mercy Medical Center, Bronx, NY.
2/11/1980	Division of Military & Naval Affairs - orders appointment as Chief Nurse, Polyclinic, Olympic Village, Lake Placid, NY.
2/29/1980	Office of the Secretary of Defense Certificate of Appreciation in support of the 1980 Olympic Winter Games.

Date/Year	Life Milestones and Important Events (not All-Inclusive)
1980	Kappa Delta Pi Honor Society, International Honor Society in Education, foster excellence in education and promote fellowship among those dedicated to teaching.
5/1/1983	Doctorate (EdD) and Master of Education (EdM) in Health Education, Columbia University, NY, 1983
8/1/1985	Senior Staff Specialist for Social and Economic Policy, August 1985 to July 1987 American Nurses Association, Corporate Headquarters, Kansas City, MO.
2/10/1986	Article - (promotion of A. Marlene Ausen to Colonel) Air Force Times "Promotion Hailed as Milestone for Air Guard."
7/1/1987	ANG Policy Advisor/Health Program, July 1987 to February 1993 Active duty, Colonel, Corporate Headquarters United States Air Force, Office of the Surgeon General, Bolling AFB, Washington, DC.
2/1/1993	ANG Assistant to the Director for Medical Readiness and Nursing Services; Brigadier General, Corporate Headquarters United States Air Force, Office of the Surgeon General, Bolling AFB, Washington, DC, February 1993 to August 1998
8/1/1993	Director, Patient Care Inspections and Program Evaluation, Office of Healthcare Inspections, VA OIG, August 1993 to July 2000.
1993	Virginia State Nurses Association, to promote advocacy and education for registered nurses to advance professional practice and influence the delivery of quality care.
3/4/1995	Honored by Teachers College, Columbia University, March 4, 1995, as a distinguished alumna and nurse for 1995

Date/Year	Life Milestones and Important Events (not All-Inclusive)
3/24/1995	VA Federal Women's Program Mentoring Recognition, for presentation at the national convention and mentoring VA employees, "Pioneering Women & Breaking the Glass Ceiling," Augusta, GA.
1/1/1996	VA Secretary's Outstanding Volunteer Service Award 1996
1/1/1997	Special Congressional Recognition Award 1997, Commendation from Mike Honda Member of Congress for service to country and serving as Grand Marshal of Veterans Day Parade, San Jose, CA, November 2007.
1/10/1997	Letter from Office of the President, Medical University of South Carolina inviting acceptance of an honorary degree Doctor of Humane Letters for contributions to the military and nursing.
2/26/1997	Letter from Office of Ass't Secretary of Defense International Security Affairs Africa Region - South African conference speaker and group luncheon meeting with Winnie Mandela.
2/27/1997	Letter from South Africa Secretary of Defence - invitation as program speaker to Conference on the Advancement of Women in the Department of Defence.
5/16/1997	Honorary Degree, Doctor of Humane Letters from the Medical University of South Carolina, May 16, 1997, for outstanding achievements in the field of nursing, the military, and the community.
9/8/1997	Letter of Recognition from Congress of the United States Congressional Black Caucus Foundation Veterans Braintrust.

Date/Year	Life Milestones and Important Events (not All-Inclusive)
10/1/1997	Women in Military Service for America Foundation (WIMSA). The Women's Memorial is a unique, living memorial honoring all military women—past, present and future. The foundation have registered over 250,000 of the 2.29 million women eligible have been registered as of January 2015.
9/1/1998	Assistant to the Director, Air National Guard (ANG) for Human Resources Readiness, Major General, (Active Reserve), Crystal City, VA, September 1998 to September 2001
1999	Sigma Theta Tau International, Honor Society for Nurses: supports the learning knowledge and development of nurses making a difference in global health.
1/1/1999	Community Mentoring Award and Tuskegee Airmen, Inc., Chapter named in my honor, at the 105th Airlift Wing, Newburgh, NY, 1999.
10/1/1999	Inducted into the Columbia University Nursing Hall of Fame October 1999
1/1/1999	Wrote brief ANG NC History published July 1993, "Highlights in the History of Air National Guard Nursing," published 1999.
1/10/1999	Letter of Acceptance to become Chapter of The Tuskegee Airmen Inc. as the Maj Gen Irene Trowell-Harris Chapter of Tuskegee Airmen, Inc.
5/10/1999	Business and Professional Women/USA, supports workforce development programs and workplace policies that recognize the diverse needs of working women, communities and businesses including veterans.

Date/Year	Life Milestones and Important Events (not All-Inclusive)
9/18/1999	Developed Mentoring Guide for ANG, "How to Implement a Military Mentoring Program: Suggested Strategies & Best Practices," published September 19, 1999.
1999	National Advisory Council, Alliance of National Defense, Advisory Board member, a positive voice for American military women.
9/28/1999	Congratulatory letter from Teachers College Columbia University - Charter Inductee into the Nursing Hall of Fame.
8/1/2000	Director, Northeast Region, Office of Healthcare Inspections, August 2000 to September 2001. Department of Veterans Affairs, Office of Inspector General (54C), Washington, DC.
6/1/2001	Honored by the Department of Epidemiology and Public Health (EPH), Yale University School of Medicine as Distinguished Alumni 2006, selected on June 1, 2001, for outstanding dedication to public service, and inducted into the EPH Public Service Honor Roll. Yale alumni chair on display at the Aiken County Historical Museum.
9/29/2001	Retired as a Major General after serving in the Air Force and Air National Guard for 38 years.
10/1/2001	Received a political appointment as Senior Service Executive at the Department of Veterans Affairs from the White House October 2001
10/1/2001	Director, Center for Women Veterans (00W), Office of the Secretary, Department of Veterans Affairs (VA), Washington, DC October 2001 to September 2013

Date/Year	Life Milestones and Important Events (not All-Inclusive)
2001	Senior Executive Association (SES) active member, an association for active and retired SES personnel and provides advocacy, resources and information for career Federal SES officers, 2001-present.
1/1/2002	Dr. James D. Weaver Society named in honor of ANG flight surgeon and distinguished PA Congressman: I received the 2002 award for my contribution to the military.
3/15/2004	Announcement as Grand Marshall 3rd (2004) Annual Black History Parade - Aiken, SC.
6/1/2004	Reagan Funeral June 04
1/1/2005	Selected as Distinguished Alumni of Teachers College, Columbia University for 2005
1/1/2005	Certificate of Appreciation VA's 75th Anniversary Celebration 2005
1/28/2005	Letter of Appreciation from Secretary of VA Anthony J. Principi.
3/15/2005	Article - Aiken Standard - "Trowell-Harris a leader for the 21st Century."
1/1/2006	Selected by Women's eNews as one of "21 Leaders for the 21st Century for 2006" in the category of "Seven Who Construct New Realities." 2006
1/1/2006	Combined Federal Campaign Recognition 2006
1/1/2006	WIMSA Wall Plaque in the Hall of Honors was given for supporting military service members and veterans, consistent donations and my accomplishment as a military officer.

Date/Year	Life Milestones and Important Events (not All-Inclusive)
4/11/2006	Letter from The Secretary of Veterans Affairs, R. James Nicholson - congratulations for being selected one of twenty-one Leaders for the 21st Century by Women's eNews.
6/2/2006	Letter regarding Distinguished Alumni Award - Yale University School of Public Health.
7/7/2006	Letter from Embry-Riddle Aeronautical University regarding visit, plaque and Eagle of Aviation Award.
9/11/2006	Letter from the founder of The Dorothy Jemison Foundation for Excellence inviting attendance as an Honored Guest for "Reality Leads Fantasy - Celebrating Women of Color in Flight."
10/1/2006	Honored October 2006 by the Dr. Mae Jemison Foundation of Excellence for contributions to aviation and mentoring.
11/1/2007	Commendation from Mike Honda, Member of Congress for service to country and serving as Grand Marshal of Veterans Day Parade, San Jose, CA, November 2007.
1/1/2008	Secretary's Award for Extraordinary Support of Voluntarism through the Combined Federal Campaign, 2008.
1/1/2008	Submitted 2008 Advisory Committee on Women Veterans Report to the Secretary and Congress.
1/1/2008	Sponsored 2008 National Summit on Women Veterans Issues.
1/1/2008	Represented the Secretary and spoke at the November 2008 Fédération Mondiale des Anciens Combattants, World Veterans Federation, Standing Committee on Women Meeting in Paris, France.

Date/Year	Life Milestones and Important Events (not All-Inclusive)
1/1/2008	The Irene Battle Trowell Memorial Education Fund with the Aiken County Historical Museum: scholarship was established in mother's memory in 2008 at the museum to educate students of Aiken County in history, especially military members and Veterans.
1/1/2009	Commendation by the Deputy Secretary of Veterans Affairs for leadership, January 2009
1/1/2009	January 2009 spent a week in Rome with sister, on an education tour of the city, Vatican, and museum.
1/1/2009	Represented (2009-2103) the Secretary of Veterans Affairs on the White House Interagency Council on Women and Girls.
2009	Represented the Secretary of Veterans Affairs as Ex-officio member of the Defense Advisory Committee on Women in the Services (DACOWITS), 2009-13. Provides advice and recommendations on servicewomen to the Secretary of Defense.
8/26/2009	Mayor's Veterans Day Parade NYC, pre-parade speaker and special guest of Mayor.
8/26/2009	Certificate of Appreciation by The Honorable Will A. Gunn, VA General Counsel for creativity in developing and sponsoring The Women's Equality Day Celebration, August 26, 2009.
9/11/2009	Letter from Aetna requesting participation in the 29th (2010) Edition of their African-American History Calendar. Recognized on the calendar in 1995 as a nurse and role model to inspire youth in SC.
1/1/2010	Publication of "Sky High: No Goal is Out of Your Reach.

Date/Year	Life Milestones and Important Events (not All-Inclusive)
11/23/2010	Contributor to: Leadership in Action	Principles Forged in the Crucible of Military Service ISBN 78-0984551163.
11/11/2012	Invitation Veterans Day White House Breakfast 2012 with photo with the President.
1/12/2013	Code of Support Foundation, COSF works to engage and leverage the full spectrum of this nation's resources to ensure that our service members, veterans, and their families receive the support they need and have earned through their service and sacrifice.
9/20/2013	Retired on September 30, 2013, from Federal service as a White House political appointee at VA after serving 25 years.
10/16/2013	The America Nurses Foundation, Friends of the National Institute of Nursing Research 2013 Gala, to honor research nurses at the Hyatt Regency Hotel on Capitol Hill, Washington, DC.
11/12/2013	Teachers College, Columbia University 125th Anniversary Gala, "Celebrating a Tradition for Tomorrow," Apollo Theater, NYC.
12/1/2013	Established an Endowed Leadership Fund at the American Nurses Foundation (ANF) to educate nurses using a systematic method to help improve the quality of care and support initiatives that give nurses a greater voice in influencing health care delivery and policy.

Date/Year	Life Milestones and Important Events (not All-Inclusive)
4/9/2014	Presented an educational session as an alumna on "My Riveting Journey: A Life in Nursing, the Military, and Government Service as a White House Appointee," at New Jersey City University to faculty, students and employees, New Jersey (life history and career progression).
4/12/2014	Academic Festival Leadership Panel Member "When Women Take the Lead" with Dr. Susan H. Fuhrman, President Teachers College, Columbia University.
4/24/2014	Attended the Service Update 2014 AFNC Senior Lamp Briefings, Office of the Air Force Surgeon General, Medical Development Facility, Fall Church, VA.
5/21/2014	Attended and marched in the Alumni Procession, Teachers College, Columbia University, Doctoral Hooding Convocation and Ceremony at the Cathedral of Saint John the Divine, NYC.
6/9/2014	Historic Holy Land Cruise, Greece, Turkey, Cyprus and Israel for 12 days with niece and friends.
7/22/2014	Attended the 25th International Nursing Research Congress - Hong Kong, China July 22 - 29, 2014
9/11/2014	Officiated event with Brig Gen Vaught at the Code of Support Foundation (COSP) "Living Wall of Honor" dedication at WIMSA for the 160 military women who died in Iraqi and in Afghanistan.
9/17/2014	Honored as "Alumna of the Year for 2014" at the Columbia Hospital School of Nurses 17th Annual Alumni Association Reunion "Celebrating Our Nursing History" in Columbia, SC

Date/Year	Life Milestones and Important Events (not All-Inclusive)
9/19/2014	Yale University Alumni Day "The Affordable Care Act" with luncheon and Awards Ceremony, New Haven Lawn Club, Conn.
10/4/2014	The keynote speaker at the National Council Negro Women, Inc. Connecticut Sections, "Honoring Military Women of Color" Hartford Windsor Marriott Hotel, Windsor, Conn.
10/15/2014	Friends of the National Institute of Nursing Research 2014 Gala," Expanding Nursing's Footprint in High Impact Research," Omni Shoreham Hotel, Washington, DC.
10/16/2014	Attended "Inspiring Global Leadership in the 21st Century" Summit at Yale University, New Haven, CT and spoke on 17 October at the Careers in Public Health Alumni Speaker Series on "Life Story and Opportunities in Public Health" at the Yale University School of Epidemiology and Public Health.
10/26/2014	23rd Annual 2014 Fall Gathering Dinner Gala "Honoring the Valor, Courage and Sacrifice of Veterans," at the Army and Navy Country Club, Arlington, VA.
11/10/2014	Honored by Business and Professional Women's (BPW) Foundation with five other outstanding military/veteran businesswomen - Keynote by First Lady, Michelle Obama.
11/11/2014	Women Veterans Rock Event, "Five Star Tribute to America's Women Veterans in Military Service," and introduced and presented award to Cathie Lechareas as the "2015 Woman Veteran of the Year," at WIMSA.

Date/Year	Life Milestones and Important Events (not All-Inclusive)
11/13/2014	Congressional Breakfast, "Returning Home: Challenges Facing Women Veterans Following Deployment" Rayburn House Office Building, DC, sponsored by Women's Policy, Inc., Disabled American Veterans and Women's Research and Education Institute.
11/19/2014	Speaker at the VA Center for Women Veterans 20th Anniversary Celebration at the Department of Veterans Affairs on "Implementing the Vision for the Center for Women Veterans."
1/23/2015	Contributor to: Glimpses of the New Veteran ISBN: 978-1-61163-708-3.
6/8/2015	Presented as keynote speaker at the Webb House, Inc. in Gary, Indiana. The program theme was "Celebration of Life."
6/17/2015	Seoul, South Korea to participate in the International Council of Nursing Summit 17-24 June.
7/23/2015	July 23-27, 2015, Attended the Honor Society of Nursing, Sigma Theta Tau International (STTI) 26th International Nursing Research Congress in San Juan, Puerto Rico. Nearly 900 nurse leaders attended the Congress representing more than thirty countries with an opportunity to network with colleagues from around globe.

Association With Organizations Spanning Years	
1963-pres	This list is not all-inclusive such as membership in AL, Kennedy Center, Smithsonian, National Assoc of Women in the Arts; life membership in 105th Airlift Wing Assoc, NGAUS, Military Assoc of NY, ROA, AFA, and NAACP.
1991-pres	Military Officers Association of America (MOAA) advocate a strong national defense and plays an active role in military personnel matters and especially proposed legislation affecting the career force, the retired community, and veterans of the uniformed service.
1999-2015	Mentored and awarded 165 TAI Tuition Assistance Scholarships ($167,000) to Hudson Valley, New Windsor, NY high school students: Maj Gen Irene Trowell-Harris Chapter of Tuskegee, Inc.
1999-2015	Mentoring is a key component of the Maj Gen Irene Trowell-Harris Chapter of Tuskegee Airmen, Inc.
1999-2015	Maj Gen Trowell-Harris Community Mentoring Award established in 1999 is given to an outstanding community person annually for mentoring.
2008-2010	VA Executive Fellows Program with Brookings Institution: Certification in Public Leadership, The Executive Summit and Leading with Integrity: Ethics in Action."
2009-2013	White House Council on Women and Girls: purpose to establish a coordinated Federal response to issues that particularly impact the lives of women and girls and to ensure that Federal programs and policies address and take into account the distinctive concerns of women and girls, including women of color and those with disabilities.

TWO INSTITUTIONS THAT PLAYED A HUGE ROLE IN MY LIFE

Mount Hill Missionary Baptist Church

They helped me build my first bridge to a new life
Mount Hill Missionary Baptist Church

An early rock in the foundation of my faith. And as I mentioned previously. The good people there, back in the days when cash was hard to come by, collected enough pennies, nickels dimes and quarters for me to make my first tuition payment to nursing school. It's safe to say my life would be vastly different if I had not been able to go to nursing school.

Martha Schofield High School -- Aiken, South Carolina

About Martha Schofield (namesake of my school as a youth in Aiken, South Carolina) and a person I greatly admire for her accomplishments.

Source: Wikipedia

A Woman with a Vision: Martha Schofield - The end of the Civil War in April of 1865 marked a time of rebuilding all over the southern part of the United States. Aiken, South Carolina was no exception.

The federally guided Reconstruction drew many people from the Northern part of the country who were prompted by their religious faith to participate. Martha Schofield, born in 1839 in Bucks County, Pennsylvania and raised as a Quaker, was one of these Northerners.

The Religious Society of Friends, also known as "Quakers," began in England in the 1600s. When Quakers first came to America, they, like other European immigrants, owned slaves. In the mid-1700s, leaders of The Friends signed a document that stated: "To bring men hither, or to rob and sell them against their will, we stand against."

Their efforts brought an end to the importation of slaves in the Northern states. By 1804, most slavery had been abolished in New England, Middle Atlantic states and the territories in the Northwest. But in the southern states, including South Carolina, slavery was still legal. The Quakers worked with other abolitionists to create a system of people and places called "The Underground Railroad" that aided slaves in escaping their captivity.

A Decision to Help Others

Martha was a young woman of 25 in 1865 when she decided to spend her life helping people who had been enslaved. Martha went to work for The Bureau of Refugees, Freedmen, and Abandoned Lands, often called "The Freedmen's Bureau." It had been created by Congress to provide food and medicine for people after the war and to establish schools, among other services. She took her life savings of little more than $400 and set out for the islands off the coast of South Carolina. Scores of former slaves had found refuge from the danger of the plantations during the war on St. Helena Island.

Many former slaves did not know how to read or write. Unfortunately, because of the tropical climate and the many diseases that are carried by mosquitoes, Martha fell ill. Wanting to continue her work and learning that Aiken offered a healthier climate, she soon moved to Aiken to teach in a place where she could recover her health.

When she arrived in Aiken in 1868, Martha bought two acres of land on the east side of today's York Street. She began work on her plans for a "Normal" school, a school that teaches students to become teachers themselves and an "Industrial" school, a school that teaches occupational skills. When the Schofield School opened in 1870, every child was taught the basic skills of reading, writing and math. However, boys learned additional skills such as how to be blacksmiths, shoemakers, and carpenters while girls were taught "home skills" like cooking and sewing. One of Schofield's students, Matilda Evans, later gained recognition throughout the country as the state's first female African-American physician.

A Successful School

The school was very successful but hard to keep afloat with meager government funds. Fundraising efforts described in school brochures from that time show that people from the north donated a significant amount. Susan B. Anthony, a famous women's suffrage leader, was one of many people who sent financial aid to Schofield School. The AME Church in Aiken also raised money and provided the support necessary to keep the doors from closing. Miss Schofield often allowed families to trade goods and services to pay for student expenses. She became a well-loved and well-respected immigrant to the South.

On the eve of her 77th birthday on February 1, 1916, Martha died in her sleep. A large birthday party had been planned to honor her remarkable life with more than 300 people attending. Instead, when it was discovered that she had died, the school bell rang to alert all of her passing.

Three days later, her casket was placed on a train car at the depot in Aiken to be sent back to her home state of Pennsylvania for burial in her family's plot. Many who had planned to celebrate her birthday were at the train depot to say goodbye to their beloved teacher. With tearful respect, the spiritual "Steal Away" began to be sung and soon the entire station was filled with a heartfelt tribute to a woman who spent her adult life pursuing her vision of helping those who had been the victims and the refugees of the Civil War.

Today, the white bell tower whose bell kept students on schedule and announced the passing of its founder is the only surviving piece of the original Schofield School.

Background Note:

Martha Fell Schofield was born February 1, 1839, near Newtown, Bucks County, PA. She was the daughter of Oliver W. Schofield and Mary (Jackson) Schofield, who were married at Darby Meeting in 1834. Both her parents were involved in a number of reform activities, including abolition, temperance, women's rights, and improved education. The family included twin older sisters, Sarah Jane and Lydia, born 1835, a brother, Benjamin, born 1837, and Eliza, a younger sister born in 1840. Of the four sisters, only Sarah Jane married, to Samuel Shinn Ash.

Martha was educated at the schools at Newtown and Byberry and the Sharon Female Seminary in Darby, Pa., which was operated by their mother's brother, John Jackson, and his wife, Rachel. Martha began her own career in teaching at age eighteen at Bayside, Long Island, New York, where her aunt, Eliza (Jackson) Bell, lived. She also taught in Harrison, Westchester Co., New York, in a school connected with Purchase Monthly Meeting.

In 1865, Martha Schofield went to the islands off the coast of South Carolina to help educate the newly freed African Americans. She found the malarial conditions devastating to her health and moved inland to Aiken, South Carolina, where she founded what became the Schofield Normal and Industrial School in 1868.

The School was partially supported by the Pennsylvania Friends Relief Association, headquartered in Germantown, Pa. and was headed by Sarah Fisher Corlies (sister of Deborah F. Wharton) and Elizabeth Dorsey. The School received some state aid for a number of years. By 1882, there were over 200 pupils, and in that year, the School was incorporated.

Need for financial aid was constant through the years, and a number of people from the Hicksite branch of Philadelphia and New York Yearly Meetings supported the school. By 1883, there were over 400 pupils who, in addition to their education, were taught a trade. In 1884, a boarding department was opened, as well as a student aid fund. In 1887, Edward Hicks Magill and Howard M. Jenkins of Swarthmore College were among those serving on the Board of Managers, and the school house was partitioned into a dormitory for boys. In 1890, the Deborah F. Wharton Industrial Hall, with half of the cost donated with by her sons, was completed.

By 1910, the school occupied two entire blocks of the town of Aiken, with three large brick buildings, two large frame buildings, and various other improvements. In addition, the school owned a 280-acre farm three miles outside of Aiken with its buildings. The running expenses were principally made up by annual gifts from voluntary subscribers. With the exception of the headmaster or headmistress and Martha Schofield, who served as Business Manager, all departments' heads and teachers were black graduates of the School.

The night before the School was to celebrate the 77th birthday of its founder, Martha Schofield died in her sleep. She died on February 1, 1916, in Aiken, S. C., and is buried in the Darby Friends burial ground in Darby, Pa. The Schofield School was absorbed into the public school system in 1952.

Scope and Content

The Schofield Normal and Industrial School was founded in 1868 by Martha Schofield (1839-1916), a Pennsylvania Quaker. Her intention initially was to provide education for freed slaves. The School gradually evolved into a boarding school for training young blacks in industrial trades or to become teachers. It was absorbed into the public school system in 1952. The collection contains minutes of the Board of Trustees (1886-1942), legal documents, financial records, correspondence and other papers.

AN ORGANIZATION I'M PROUD TO BE AFFILIATED WITH:

THE TUSKEGEE AIRMEN, INC.

The 'Red Tails' and What They Meant

This chapter is not about me but is about something and a group of men I'm very proud of. It touches on something that people of all races and ethnic backgrounds should wish to emulate and certainly must respect.

There is a recurring theme in the background of some of the most successful people in all areas of human endeavors. Adversity and overcoming it. They overcame the challenges, the obstacles, and the barriers that they were faced with. That above all deserves honor and respect.

In the early days of World War II, there was a group of men that individually and collectively faced everything that centuries-old racist thinking and stereotyping could throw at them—just so they could fight for the very country that thought them incapable.

It took the United States Congress in 1941 to force the Army Air Corps to form an African-American combat unit. On March 19, 1941, the 99th Pursuit Squadron ("Pursuit" being the pre-World War II term for what would become "Fighter") was activated. It in turn became the core to form other squadrons.

In June 1941, the Tuskegee program officially began with the formation of the 99th Fighter Squadron at the Tuskegee Institute. The War Department's efforts to derail the formation of the combat unit consisted of establishing very high requirements for higher education and flight experience. They felt safe since they did not believe any African-American men would be able to meet those requirements. The Tuskegee Institute had participated in the Civilian Pilot Training Program since 1939 and many African-American men had taken part in it. Thanks to the quality of the education and training program at the Tuskegee Institute, the War Department's plan backfired. The Air Corps received more than enough applications from men who qualified—meeting the high bar of entry.

The Tuskegee Airmen story is about men who rose above adversity and discrimination and opened a door once closed to black America. Before the Tuskegee Airmen, no African-American combat units or military pilots existed. The Tuskegee Airmen went on to serve honorably throughout WWII becoming one of its most highly decorated units.

Today there are fifty-five chapters of the Tuskegee Airmen, Inc. (TAI) that honor the memory of the Tuskegee Airmen and what they stood for.

About the Major General Irene Trowell-Harris Chapter of Tuskegee Airmen

Chaplain (Lt. Col.) Julius Jefferson of the 105th Airlift Wing, a former Stewart Air National Guard Base member, went to the Tuskegee Airmen, Inc. (TAI) convention in Kansas City. And was so inspired that he asked about forming a chapter at Stewart Air National Guard Base (ANGB). The Stewart Chapter of TAI was named in my honor and that recognition humbles me. The Major General Irene Trowell-Harris Chapter of TAI was organized on January 10, 1998, at Stewart ANGB in Newburgh, New York. It was named for me based on my accomplishments as the first African-American female two-star general in the 359-year history of the National Guard and the first woman and nurse in Air National

Guard history to command a medical clinic. But I could not have accomplished some of the things I did while in the military if the Tuskegee Airmen had not blazed a trail for me by their efforts and desire to fight for their country. And then by excelling once they were able to.

MAJOR GENERAL IRENE TROWELL-HARRIS CHAPTER
NEWBURGH, NY

The primary goal of the Major General Irene Trowell-Harris Chapter of Tuskegee Airmen, Inc. is to promote the interest and honor the memory of the men and the women who served in the Army Air Corp at Tuskegee Alabama during the 1940s. Our chapter will accomplish this by promoting the Tuskegee Airmen at various functions throughout the year, and in our everyday activities as chapter members. In doing so, we will teach the aspiration, frustrations and successes of these pioneering men and women in the United States Army Air Corp at Tuskegee, Alabama. We will strive to keep their legacy alive.

As a Chapter, we will continue to provide financial assistance to the National Scholarship Fund and the Historical Museum Fund. Also, we will continue our Major General Irene Trowell-Harris Chapter Tuition Assistance Dinner Dance to support our local college-bound students. Additionally, we plan to become one of the leading Tuskegee Airmen chapters providing positive, successful, energetic and ambitious mentors to young men and women.

Our Chapter will take an active role in the community. We realize that our local community must be involved in our progress and so we will actively recruit them to the organization. We will do so by asking for their involvement both physically and financially. For the Major General Irene Trowell-Harris Chapter to be viable, we must incorporate the community in our leadership and membership.

The chapter seeks to develop and implement a pilot enrichment program where students of any age group might be provided a way into the world of aviation. We want to expose young students to aviation, whether as pilots, mechanics or engineers. We will provide the discipline, knowledge and the mentors needed to broaden their knowledge of aviation. This will bring great credit to an organization that strives for excellence. These are some of the goals of the Major General Irene Trowell-Harris Chapter. They are consistent with that of the National Organization of Tuskegee Airmen, Inc.

This superb effort has made it possible to award $167,000 in scholarships to 165 Hudson Valley seniors since 1997.

During 2014, the chapter president participated in numerous speaking engagements to local youth groups and organizations and represented the chapter at various community events. These commitments included: over 400 mentor hours to the Red Tail Youth Flying Program annually, participated in various charitable events, the Willie Carter Golf Classic raising money for the scholarship program, and Family Day in the Park giving back to community assisted by 105th AW. Also, the Hudson Valley

Tuskegee Airmen Endowment Fund raises money for our future scholarship program through the Orange/Sullivan Community Foundation. These events continue to highlight a national need for mentorship and sponsorship for our youth as future leaders.

I am proud of the hard work that our members have done to make these scholarships possible, but I am even more proud of the trailblazing Tuskegee Airmen and what they have achieved for America.

I would like to share with you some of what the mission of Tuskegee Airmen, Inc. (TAI) is:

- To foster recognition of, and preserve the history of African-American achievement in aviation.

- To inspire and motivate young men and women toward endeavors in aviation and aerospace careers. In essence, to mentor and build bridges for young students nationally.

- To bring together in a spirit of friendship and goodwill, all persons who share the aspirations and successes of men and women who pioneered in military aviation and in the Tuskegee experiment.

In addition, TAI National programs:

- Administer youth aviation programs

- Provide mentors and role models

- Perform community outreach and mentoring

- Make nominations to service academies

- Do historical research

Specifically, my namesake Chapter's goals are:

- To promote the interests and honor the memories of the men and women who served in the Army Air Corps at Tuskegee Alabama during the 1940s.

- To continue to provide financial assistance to the National Scholarship Fund and the Historic Museum Fund.

- To continue to sponsor the Annual Major General Irene Trowell-Harris Chapter Tuition Assistance Award Celebration; this provides scholarships to local college-bound students.

- To become one of the leading Tuskegee Airmen Chapters by providing positive and ambitious mentors to young men and women.

- To create a pilot enrichment program; this will expose students to the aviation career field.

In pursuit of these goals, the chapter will continue to forge partnerships with community leaders who possess information and knowledge consistent with chapter goals. The section realizes that the local community is imperative to the organization's progress.

The Lee A. Archer, Jr. Red Tail Youth Flying Program was started on October 6, 2001. This program provides instruction and mentoring primarily low to middle-income youth that would not normally have the opportunity to attend flight school or have an aviation, mentor. We are proud of this one of a kind program that gives students an opportunity to receive their private pilot licenses, as they become seniors in high school.

The chapter hosts the Annual Willie Carter Golf Classic. Willie Carter is a local golf pro who has been touching the lives of many people through his golf clinics, schools, and pro shop. He is a former principal at a local elementary school and is a businessman. He was selected as the recipient of the Major General Irene Trowell-Harris Chapter of Tuskegee Airmen, Inc. Community mentoring award for his work with youth and the community.

The chapter hosts a dinner annually in February to award scholarships and help sponsor a family day during the summer in Newburgh, New York. We will continue to build on the successes of these and other programs to make the Trowell-Harris Chapter the premier chapter of Tuskegee Airmen, Inc.

In addition, the Chapter will continually promote the rich history of the Tuskegee Airmen and honor those Red Tails still among us. Whether during chapter-sponsored functions or in everyday activities as chapter members, we will herald the outstanding achievements and spirit of the Tuskegee Airmen.

MG Irene Trowell-Harris Chapter,
 Tuskegee Airmen, Inc.
One Maguire Way
Stewart ANGB
Newburgh, NY 12550-5076
Tel: (845) 838-7848
Fax: (845) 567-1731
Email: TAI_NY@hotmail.com
www.TAI-NY.org

Major General Irene Trowell-Harris Chapter
Tuition Assistance Award Recipients

1999	Curtis Bodison
	Marques Grant
	Amon Croston

2000	Shannon Williams
	Candice Barnett
	Kasaine Ole Pertet
	Ronnie Fisher

2001	Alicia Beckwith
	Desiree Lucas
	Shauntey Jones
	Jilian Martarano
	Amber Ponder
	Robert Rogers III

2002	Lydia Underwood
	Tiara Oliver
	Jose Burgos
	Joy Romulus
	Nadine Brooks
	Ashley Wimes
	Rossmary Gill

2003	Bryan Vivaldo
	Florence Evina-Ze
	Giovanni Holman
	Melanie Dyer-Cabrera
	Nia Cooper
	Abby Mennerich
	Matthew Kenney

2004	Corinne Mitchell
	Erik Hillard
	Piotr Waksmundski
	Kristen O'Donnell
	Shtoya Jones
	Calvin Perez
	Joseph Urciuoli
	William Cappola, Jr.
	Frankie Brown
	Marinancy Rocha

2005	Antoine Crudup
	Andrea Mattracio
	Nathan Nicoiato
	Kathryn Rittweger
	Jennifer Traditi
	Fiorella Uene
	Jessica Riccardi
	Aaliya McClinton
	Kennen Butleer
	Sajjad Abdullateef
	Jordan Casson

2006	Mara Phelan
	Tanisha Younger
	Lyndsay LaBarge
	Tiara Williamson
	Ruthann Brereton
	Danielle Rivera
	Jason Fleischer
	Joshua O. Davis
	Mariela Vidal
	Leslie Caesar II
	Antonio Roma
	Bruno S. Frustace

2007	Carly Butwell
	Sonja Bostick
	Benjamin Harris
	Heather Heidelberg
	Cherish Hunt
	Doniella McKoy
	Nikhil Menon
	Alicia Oakley
	Evan Pritchard
	Joseph Parrelli
	Leonel Soriano
	Steven Traditi

2008	Jeff Arndt
	Austin Brochetti
	Miriah Fountain

Dr. Irene Trowell-Harris

Caitlyn Hitt
Michelle Grantt
Richard Mitchell
Miriam Montes
Nia Newton
Candice Otero
Laisa Pertet
Paris West

2009
Jessica Aumick
Michelle Lemieux
Shanicee Mckoy
Janay N. Ware
Alray K. Cromer
Gina Marie Melendez
Robert C. Dana
Rian Howard
Kelly Sticca
Aleen Coughlin

2010
Matthew Farmer
Naja Fandal
Leon Williams
Gianni Perez
David Piazza
Christopher Colas
Andre Marin
Pavel Salnikov
Katherine Dunham
Klonet Johnson

2011
Gregory Shilling
Aaaron Perez
Dominique Whisnant
Matthew Fama
Raul Castillo
Monserrat Duran
Jodi-Kaye Haber
Herbert Koomson
Sohrob Sullivan-Davachi
Charisse Bruce

2012
Katelyn Anderson
Kelly Boamah
Connor Gray
Pierce Johnston

Dwight Mariano
Maya Lawson
Teresa Peralta
Allison Rondash
Ilci Velarde
Jeremy Velazquez

2013
Kristopher Buck
William Espana
Shabab Hussain
Jonathan Iglesias
Patrick Junjulas
Tiffany Lok
Tamika Oliver
Alexis Peterson
Alexandra Williams
Richard Zhunio

2014
Lauren Maitner
Simonne Cazoe
Jerome Mckeever
Amanda Lugo
Elijio Cruz
Thomas O'connell
Bhavana Patil
Cinthia Cordoba
Sharleen Lima
Junus Sela
Neomi L. Brereton
Olivia Avery

2015
Steven Branche
Ashley Cassamir
Taylor Chappel
Julia Delgado
Justin Leathers
Jenny Ly
David Mejia
Jennifer Ortiz
Dominick Peluso
Daryl Riley
Darab Sullivan-Davachi

ABOUT THE AUTHOR

Dr. Irene Trowell-Harris is the former Director of the Department of Veterans Affairs (VA) Center for Women Veterans. She was nominated in June 2001 and approved by the White House on October 2, 2001, and served as director until September 2013. In this role, she was the primary advisor to the Secretary of Veterans Affairs on legislation, programs, and issues related to women Veterans. Prior to her appointment, Dr. Trowell-Harris served as Director of VA's Office of Inspector General's Healthcare Inspections Regional Office in Washington DC. In this position, she directed a multidisciplinary staff of inspectors responsible for conducting oversight reviews to improve the economy, effectiveness, and efficiency of VA's programs.

Concurrent with her position in VA's Office of Inspector General, Dr. Trowell-Harris served 38 years in the United States Air Force and ANG, retiring as a Major General in September 2001. During her military career, Dr. Trowell-Harris held numerous senior leadership positions, including: chief nurse executive; Flight Nurse Examiner; commander; advisor for nursing and readiness, Office of the AF Surgeon General, assistant to the director and Board of Directors, ANG; and military representative to the Defense Advisory Committee on Women in the Services (DACOWITS) for the ANG. She was a 1997 Air Force representative for the Committee on Women in the NATO Forces Conference held in Istanbul, Turkey and speaker for the Air Force in Pretoria, South Africa at an International Women's Conference.

Dr. Trowell-Harris is an adjunct graduate faculty member at the Uniformed Services University of the Health Sciences and served as an ex-officio member to the DACOWITS and VA's representative on the White House Council on Women and Girls. She also served as a senior social and policy specialist for the American Nurses Association.

Born in Aiken, S.C., Dr. Trowell-Harris is a graduate of Columbia Hospital School of Nursing, Jersey City State University, where she earned a bachelor's degree with honors in health education. She received a master's degree in Public Health from Yale University and a doctorate in education from Teachers College, Columbia University.

Dr. Trowell-Harris was the first female and nurse to command a medical clinic and first African-American woman in the history of the National Guard to be promoted to General Officer. She is also the first to have a mentoring award and a Tuskegee Airmen, Inc., Chapter named in her honor.

Dr. Trowell-Harris is the recipient of numerous awards, most notably the Air Force Distinguished Service and Legion of Merit awards; the Dr. James D. Weaver Society Award, named for the distinguished Pennsylvania Congressman and Air National Guard Flight Surgeon; the Eagle Award from Embry-Riddle Aeronautical University for her contributions to aviation; the Air Force Association's National Aerospace Award for Department of Veterans Affairs Employee of the Year 2010, given for the most outstanding performance of duty as a VA employee and her consistent dedication to the well-being of our Veterans, the VA Outstanding and Invaluable Service to the Community Award; and numerous Outstanding Performance awards. She is a Distinguished Alumna of Jersey City State University, Yale University and Columbia University, and was inducted into the Columbia University Nursing Hall of Fame and the Yale University School of

Medicine Honor Roll for her dedication to public service. She was honored as one of the "21 Leaders of the 21st Century" by Women's eNews in NYC and was selected October 2014 by the Business and Professional Women's Foundation as a National Business Women's Week award recipient for 2014 as a decorated military veteran and veterans advocate.

She is a Charter Member of the Women's Memorial and in December 2013 established the Dr. Irene Trowell-Harris Endowed Leadership Fund at the American Nurses Foundation. The purpose of the Fund is to support leadership development of nurses – especially those with military experience and in non-traditional roles.

Publications

Author: ***Sky High: No Goal is Out of Your Reach,*** Adducent: Veterans Publishing System, an imprint from Adducent, Jacksonville, FL, 2010.

Contributor to: ***Leadership in Action | Principles Forged in the Crucible of Military Service Can Lead Corporate America Back to the Top***

By: Greg Slavonic, Rear Admiral, USN, Ret.

ISBN978-0-9845511-7-0

Published by Fortis, a nonfiction imprint from Adducent, Jacksonville, FL, 2010.

Other Contributors: General David Petraeus, USA, Lt. Gen. Don Wetekam, USAF (Ret); Rear Admiral Doug McClain, USN; Rear

Admiral Tom Zelibor, USN (Ret); Captain Tom Hudner, USN, (Ret); Major General Irene Trowell-Harris, USAF (Ret); Colonel David Scott, USAF (Ret); Colonel Wesley Fox, USMC (Ret); Colonel Chuck DeBellevue, USAF (Ret); Commander Dan O'Shea, USN; Tom Faught, USMC, former Assistant Secretary of the Navy. Plus, chapters are written about Cmdr. Lloyd "Pete" Bucher, USN (Ret) by Lt. "Skip" Schumacher, his Operations Officer aboard the USS Pueblo (AGER-2). And by Lt. Colonel Jim Zumwalt, USMC (Ret) on his father, Admiral Elmo Zumwalt. And, finally for a unique chapter written on Capt. John Paul Jones by Rear Admiral Joe Callo, USNR (Ret).

About the Book: Our country has witnessed leadership successes and failures, some large some small, at different times throughout its history. Much like what an individual experiences throughout their life—we all have bad times and good times. Our most recent "bad times" highlight so strongly a number of leadership failures that led to them—that books like this one are necessary.

This book provides the reader with a collection of highly successful real-world leaders. Each detailing their own sound fundamental principles on how to lead, what to do as a leader and most importantly—how not to lose sight of the objective of the mission. Corporate America and leaders (or those who want to become more effective leaders) of businesses of all sizes and kinds can learn much from the experiences and guidance shared in this book. There are fewer things more complicated and high-risk than responsibility for the men and women in our military and our relationship with other nations.

No matter the branch, much of the time even routine daily tasks bring with them the reality of people in life or death situations. On the international scene, small errors and incidents are magnified, often having outsized consequences. To lead in this environment and succeed at the highest levels, takes uncommon courage and skill. To say it is challenging would be an understatement. This book shares details of the men and women who rose to the challenge. In the reading, you can learn from them transferable skills and qualities that will have just as much success in the business world as they have proven in the military. Those who contributed to this book would rightly be a "Who's Who" list of our nation's most highly honored and decorated military leaders. Two-, three- and four-star Generals, Admirals, Captains, Colonels and Commanders; war heroes and two Medal of Honor recipients—they know what it takes to lead and to succeed.

Contributor to: ***Glimpses of the New Veteran***

Changed Constituencies, Different Disabilities, and Evolving Resolutions

Edited by Alice A. Booher

ISBN: 978-1-61163-708-3

About the Book: Glimpses of the New Veteran addresses three premises:(1) the veteran constituency has changed with use of an all-volunteer force, Guard, Reserves, women, aging veterans, etc.; (2) veterans' disabilities and treatments for disease and injuries have changed; and, (3) while traditional veterans-oriented programs may be strained, for whatever reasons, all of us in the community, in and out of government, whether veterans, service officers, caregivers, family, lawyers, physicians, social workers, etc., can uniquely and substantively assist in resolving these shared concerns.

The book's intent is not to criticize time-honored resources, and it does not try to be either a handbook or manual, but, rather, it provides increased understanding and food for thought. The authors, all experts in veteran's law and/or medicine, policymakers, judges, lawyers, physicians, soldiers ranging from Generals to Enlisted personnel, Reserves, National Guard, and wounded warriors. They explore these changes from their own wide spectrum of experiences; and they present viable alternatives for the twenty-first century, from official benefits processes at state and national levels and employment, training opportunities, and veterans treatment courts to blue-ribbon examples of efforts from nonprofits and corporations and pro Bono work from law firms, that are now operational and effective and may be increasingly viable and adaptable for the future.

Contributing authors include: Judie Armington, Lee Becker, Alice Booher, David Coker, Rhonda Cornum, Kory Cornum, Paul Galanti, William Gunnar, Carolyn Haug, Terry Howell, Marti Nell Hyland, Anthony Mainelli, Lory Manning, Lawrence Miller, James Ridgway, Ron Smith, Roy Spicer, James Terry, Irene Trowell-Harris, James Weiskopf, Richard Williams and Aragorn Thor Wold.

SELECT SPEECHES & PRESENTATIONS

Brief Motivational Presentation TAI Event 7 Feb 2015

The 17th Annual Tuition Assistance Awards Celebration and Dinner Dance

Good Evening,

Senior leaders, distinguished guests, service members, veterans, ladies, and gentlemen. I am honored to welcome you to the Major General Irene Trowell-Harris Chapter of Tuskegee Airmen, Inc. (TAI) 17th Annual Tuition Assistance Awards Celebration. This years' theme, **"Climb High, Dream Higher... Attitude Determines Altitude,"** is most relevant as we continue to fulfill the Chapter's charter to mentor our youth and honor the enduring legacy of the Tuskegee Airmen.

Your continuous support has made it possible for this chapter to award $167,000 in scholarships to 165 Hudson Valley seniors since 1997. This type of success takes a village. Regardless of your role here tonight whether as sponsor, exhibitor, university faculty; servicemember, veteran, business, community; education, religious or political representative and other supporters, you are doing your part to pay it forward for future generations of leaders.

By your presence here tonight, each of you have purchased a ticket on the education train with its destination leadership station. These scholarship recipients have excelled and are on that train to success with their destination leadership station. You have given them the opportunity to Climb High and Dream Higher. You can take pride in the role you're played in their journey toward success.

My story is an example of a community working together to pay it forward for future generations. I grew up on a small cotton farm in Aiken, South Carolina with 10 sisters and brothers. I graduated from high school with honors and had participated in numerous extracurricular activities. My desire was to attend college; however, I did not have the funds. When I informed my church elder of my need for college tuition – the next Sunday community members collected sixty dollars in dimes, nickels, and quarters for my nursing school tuition. There was not one paper dollar in the basket, just loose change.

That year I entered nursing school and subsequently graduated with honors. A few years later I was admitted to Yale University with a full scholarship and a stipend earning a Master Degree in Public Health and subsequently earned a doctorate from Columbia University in Health Education. With this education I was able to earn senior Flight Nurse wings, 2 stars, and a doctorate, wrote two books, and became a White House political appointee as an SES member at the Department of Veterans Affairs serving two presidents.

Even though my career flight made unscheduled stops, ran into turbulence, reached unexpected heights and traveled internationally, I was able to achieve my dreams. So you see what community support with $60.00 can do!

In retrospect during my career, I must have said to myself, "Climb High, Dream Higher… Attitude Determines Altitude." Now I am paying it forward for the next generation by my participation in nine (9) education, scholarship, and mentoring initiatives.

Thank you again for supporting this event and paying tribute to the invaluable contributions of those Tuskegee Airmen, who have served our country so admirably. Their accomplishments and ability to triumph over adversity serve as a model for all to emulate.

Together, we have made remarkable strides in paying it forward for future generations.

Tonight, I offer my congratulations to the scholarship award recipients.

As you move forward in your career - do not necessarily follow where the path may lead, but go boldly where there is no path and leave a trail.

My message to you tonight is to:

- Sit at the front of the room,
- Listen to the message,
- Take notes.

Because the WORLD is waiting... spread your wings and soar like an eagle to success!

Thank you.

Dr. Irene Trowell-Harris, RN, EdD
Maj Gen, USAF, Retired

Commencement Ceremony Remarks, 15 May 2014, New Jersey City University, Jersey City, New Jersey

Good Morning,

President Henderson, members of the Board of Trustees, distinguished faculty, parents, and the class of 2014. It is indeed a pleasure for me to be here this morning. Thank you for inviting me to make remarks at your Commencement Ceremony.

First, to the Board of Trustees - thank you for giving me the privilege of receiving this Honorary Doctorate of Humane Letters as well as the chance to be part of this wonderful day at NJCU.

Today, I offer my congratulations to the class of 2014.

Remember that the future is the bright light ahead of you. Walk toward that light, and enjoy your journey. Walt Disney stated this point succinctly when he said:

> *Keep moving forward,*
> *Opening new doors,*
> *And doing new things....*
>
> *Your curiosity will lead you down a path of success.*

My advice - don't let anyone define who you are. What you can conceive in your mind, believe in your heart, you can achieve with your efforts! Nothing is impossible! It's just the degree of difficulty! You may not be able to change the world, but you can shine a light where you are.

My story is an example: In a cotton field in South Carolina many years ago, I had a vision and dream. When I was about 15, I observed an airplane flying over and said to my 10 sisters and brothers – one day I will work and teach on an airplane. At that time in history, this was an unattainable dream with many barriers. In spite of the barriers, I still wanted flight wings.

At this point, I was graduating from high school and did not have tuition for nursing school or college. When I informed my church elder of the need for funds – the next Sunday community members collect sixty dollars in dimes, nickels, and quarters for my nursing school tuition. I was admitted and graduated from nursing school with honors and obtained immediate employment.

Ten years after that day, standing in the cotton field, watching that plane climb high in the sky; I proudly walked upon the stage and accepted my silver Flight Nurse wings at the Aerospace School of Medicine, Flight Nurse Branch, Brooks Air Force Base, San Antonio, Texas. This was one of my most cherished accomplishments! A few years later I decided to return to college for a degree here NJCU. I received a world-class education, enjoyed the university environment, the diversity of students, nursing colleagues, and music classes.

While at the University my colleagues and I frequently discussed possibly attending graduate school and seeking nursing positions with more responsibility. As we discussed this option, a faculty member suggested that we check the bulletin board each day for possible scholarship opportunities. A few months prior to graduation from NJCU, I noticed a brochure from Yale University on the bulletin board offering graduate scholarships for students in numerous professional areas.

I called for additional information related to the Public Health program (MPH), visited Yale, talked to numerous faculty members and students, and then applied officially for admission. I was subsequently admitted to the Master of Public Health program at Yale University with a full scholarship and a stipend for two years.

Note that I learned of the Yale University opportunity while enrolled NJCU. Also, it was this university that inspired and helped me obtain a bridge to graduate school. Because of this experience I went on to earn a doctorate at Columbia University.

Even though, my career flight made unscheduled stops, ran into turbulence, reached unexpected heights and traveled internationally I was able to achieve my dreams. So you see nothing is impossible! It's just the degree of difficulty!

Today is about you the students - as you graduate from New Jersey City University, remember that your degree is a symbol of:

- the new knowledge you have gained,
- the goals you have set and achieved,
- the new friendships you have made, and
- the more knowledgeable person you have become.

Hold on to your memories and be proud of your accomplishments.

Follow your dream - if you stumble, don't stop and lose sight of your goal, press on; your goal is to become successful.

Eleanor Roosevelt illustrated this point when she said, "The future belongs to those who believe in the beauty of their dreams."

Today is about more than just your graduation.

- Today is a celebration of the life you're living,
- The discoveries you're making,
- The challenges you're meeting,
- And this is more than a wish for a happy day, it's a celebration of the beautiful person you are.

Tomorrow's dreams will blossom from the seeds you sore today. May you fulfill every dream in your heart. May you reach every goal you pursue. And may this special day be only the start of a bright, happy future for you.

In addition to celebrating your accomplishments as graduates – chart your course to:

- Move ahead, but not so fast that you cannot smell the flowers;
- Stay focused, but turning aside to help someone in need;
- Take a bow, but applauding those who had a part in your success, your parents, faculty members, and other supporters.

As you move forward in your career - do not necessarily follow where the path may lead, but go boldly where there is no path and leave a trail.

In summary, to the class of 2014 - The WORLD is waiting - spread your wings and soar like an eagle to success!

Thank you.

Dr. Irene Trowell-Harris, RN, EdD
Major General, USAF, Retired

Yale University, Department of Epidemiology and Public Health, School of Medicine, New Haven, CT

2006 Distinguished Alumni Award
June 2, 2006

Good Afternoon,

Dr. Steele, Dr. Cleary, Ms. Addiss, Ms. Anderson, faculty members, ladies, and gentlemen. It is indeed a pleasure for me to be here this afternoon. I thank the Association of Yale Alumni in Public Health (AYAPH) Award Committee for selecting me as the recipient of the 2006 Distinguished Alumna Award. The telephone call informing me of the award rendered me speechless and I consider this a distinct honor.

I will address my career and public health challenges related to my journey and how I used these experiences to mentor and inspire others.

Even though we are dealing with public health challenges of the 21st century, let's go back a few years in time to the 20th century. I was delivered by a midwife on a small cotton farm shared with 10 brothers and sisters in Aiken, South Carolina.

We did not have health insurance, running water, indoor plumbing, an expensive house, a bank account, or any of the material things that usually signify the "American Dream," but we had, two parents - a mother and father - a loving home, a good religious foundation, a sense of caring for each other, and support from the entire community. You clearly recognize the public health challenges from the beginning of my career journey.

I realized early that we lacked health insurance, which can be a life-saving commodity. This meant that we did not have access and could only seek health care if we were bleeding or in severe pain. In conversation with my dentist, his nurse, and others, they informed me that the key was education and economics. These professionals said that if you get a good education, you could get a job, health insurance, a house with running water and indoor plumbing. These were major public health challenges for my family and the community.

The question for me was what should be done? I did not have the answer.

However, this journey began when my church and high school united to share their financial resources with me by providing a scholarship for nursing school. My church collected $60.00 in nickels, dimes, and quarters for my initial tuition for nursing school. The church provided the bridge I needed to get from the cotton field to college. When I graduated, I invested in the human potential stock market instead of that sports car, new clothes, and a stereo. That was in the 1960s.

I shared my resources with my 10 sisters and brothers to help them get their college degrees or start small businesses. One went to medical school and became an Air Force Flight Surgeon, another a pilot, others completed degrees in nursing and social science, and three are successful small business owners in Aiken, South Carolina. Family values, unity, and support from the entire community clearly empowered us to become successful.

Let me tell you about my journey. You see, as a young woman, I took an uncharted flight from the cotton fields of South Carolina to the pinnacle of success as a registered nurse, senior executive, educator, mentor, role model, and military officer. This flight made unscheduled stops, ran into turbulence, reached unexpected heights, and traveled internationally. Even involvement in a plane crash early in my career did not discourage me from my goal.

Just like many of you - I had a dream and vision. In that cotton field in the late 1950s, I saw an airplane flying over and I said to my 10 sisters and brothers - one day I will teach and work on an airplane - we all laughed - because we knew that was an impossible dream for a minority female! In spite of the barriers, I still wanted silver wings.

Ten years later, I proudly walked across the stage and accepted my silver Flight Nurse wings from the Aerospace School of Medicine, Flight Nurse Branch at Brooks Air Force Base in San Antonio, Texas. This was one of my most cherished accomplishments.

Even though my dream to fly was realized, like many others, I have experienced my share of challenges, obstacles and disappointments. Just like others, I delivered newspapers and worked in fast food restaurants.

The Air National Guard helped me realize my dream to fly. Guard leaders mentored me, nurtured me, educated me, and offered me many challenging opportunities.

I had the opportunity to serve my country in numerous senior executive positions, both in the military and civilian sectors. I retired as a Major General in September 2001 after serving in the Air Force and Air National Guard for 38 years, 5 months, 26 days and 3 hours.

The United States Air Force core values helped me to sustain my performance. The core values are:

- Integrity First
- Service Before Self, and
- Excellence in All We Do

As General Michael E. Ryan noted, these values inspire the trust, which provides the unbreakable bond that unifies the force.

Admission to Yale University Department of Epidemiology and Public Health was the turning point in my life – a new dimension and level that I would have considered unimaginable and unattainable a few years earlier! I had the opportunity to learn and work with the best and brightest minds in the world, faculty and students, which expanded my horizon.

As my career progressed I was able to achieve:

- Senior Flight Nurse wings
- Masters from Yale and a doctorate from Columbia
- Promotion to the rank of Major General (2-stars) in the United States Air Force and Air National Guard
- White House political appointment to the Department of Veterans Affairs
- Placed in the Yale University School of Medicine Honor Roll for dedication to public service
- Inducted into Teachers College, Columbia University Nursing Hall of Fame
- Tuskegee Airmen, Inc. chapter named in honor
- Community Mentoring Award named in honor
- Selected by Women's eNews as one of twenty-one Leaders for the 21st Century for 2006 in the category of "Seven Who Construct New Realities." I was honored in NYC May 16, 2006, and recently the
- Embry-Riddle Aeronautical University, Aviation Eagle Award

I mention these accomplishments to remind others that, even though you may come from humble beginnings, you can be successful beyond your expectations. However, let us not forget - I did not accomplish these goals alone - pioneers chartered the course and I simply followed the path extending it just a little to realize my dream. You young people out there will extend this path to immeasurable heights and distances because you are destined yet for higher roles and greatness! While we have made monumental advances, there is no time to rest on our laurels. We still have a lot of work to do. Today, my family has health insurance, but I am most concerned about the nearly 46 million Americans who do not.

As a leader, I was educated to inspire, share, and mentor others along the way. You see my accomplishments must be used to benefit society. And specifically, to inspire, mentor, improve the quality of life for families including veterans and military members, and serve our country. Thus improving the educational and economic status of our citizens, which hopefully ultimately results in positive health behavior and good public health practices. Success is measured not only in achievement, but also, in lessons learned, lives touched, and moments shared along the way.

Your spirit comes alive when you have the courage to follow a dream, to create change, to do what is right over what is easy, and the courage to value tomorrow as much as you do today. That's what helps you to create a memorable life.

I will continue to champion opportunities for collaboration to enhance public health practices. This includes working with:

- The Department of Defense
- The Congress
- Coordination with representatives in the fifty-four states and territories through the governor's office

- National veterans service organizations, women, minority and political groups
- Other federal agencies and private organizations
- Various universities

I will continue to serve on numerous policy boards and committees addressing issues with respect to healthcare disparities, education, research, housing, mentoring, diversity, and obesity and diabetes initiatives.

There have been many good times and a few bad times - however, in the bad times I am reminded of Maya Angelou's poem, which inspired new hope in many Americans. She said: "History, despite its wrenching pain, cannot be unlived, but if faced with courage, need not be lived again."

My advice is to follow your dreams - if you stumble, don't stop and lose sight of your goal, press on. Your goal is to become successful. Eleanor Roosevelt illustrated this point when she said, "The future belongs to those who believe in the beauty of their dreams."

Remember that you are successful the moment you start moving toward a worthwhile goal. Winston Churchill said, "Success is never final. Failure is never fatal. It is the courage that counts." Never stop striving and growing, because there are difficult challenges that await you as we move into the 21st century.

The question this afternoon is how can we systematically inspire the masses of young women and men to vigorously pursue their goals and reach their potential? I don't know the answer - but we must care about young people because they are our future leaders.

Dr. Martin Luther King said that we must care about each other because:

"We are bound together in an inescapable network of mutuality, tied in a single garment of destiny. Whatever affects one directly affects all indirectly."

Today we face some grave challenges with national and international world crises such as lack of health care, the potential for bird flu, global warming, and the War on Terrorism. In spite of these challenges, we must work together globally as a team to resolve these concerns and take care of our citizens. Do we have the intelligence, humor, imagination, courage, tolerance, love, respect, and willpower to meet these challenges? I say yes because it is the human spirit that will propel us to success:

- Money cannot buy it,
- Power cannot compel it,
- Technology cannot create it,
- It can only come from the human spirit!

Forty-five years ago, President John F. Kenney gave a call for public service. He said, "And so my fellow Americans - ask not what your country can do for you, but what you can do for your country." Today I say, "Ask not what public health can do for you, but what you can do to advance public health practices for our citizens nationally and internationally."

In closing, in of spite political challenges I ask you today to seize the moment, accept the challenge, because EACH of you can make a difference - and remember if it is to be - it is up to you and me!

Dr. Irene Trowell-Harris

Maj Gen, USAF, Retired, RN, MPH, EdD

www.ingramcontent.com/pod-product-compliance
Lightning Source LLC
Chambersburg PA
CBHW040223110426

42813CB00036B/3460/J